"Lavender and Cavaiola have produced a workbook that guides the reader in self-exploration and suggests ways to maintain positive self-esteem when in relationships with difficult people. The authors present easy-to-understand definitions, descriptions, and activities focused on essentials that help the reader."

—Nina W. Brown, Ed.D., LPC, NCC, FAGPA, professor and eminent scholar at Old Dominion University in Norfolk, VA

THE
ONE-WAY
Relationship
WORKBOOK

Step-by-Step Help for Coping with

Narcissists, Egotistical Lovers,

Toxic Coworkers & Others Who

Are Incredibly **Self-Absorbed**

NEIL J. LAVENDER, PH.D.
ALAN CAVAIOLA, PH.D.

New Harbinger Publications, Inc.

Distributed in Canada by Raincoast Books

Copyright © 2010 by Neil J. Lavender and Alan Cavaiola
New Harbinger Publications, Inc.
5674 Shattuck Avenue
Oakland, CA 94609
www.newharbinger.com

All Rights Reserved
Printed in the United States of America

Acquired by Jess O'Brien; Cover design by Amy Shoup;
Edited by Brady Kahn; Text design by Tracy Carlson

Library of Congress Cataloging-in-Publication Data

Lavender, Neil J.
 The one-way relationship workbook : step-by-step help for coping with narcissists, egotistical lovers, toxic coworkers, and others who are incredibly self-absorbed / Neil J. Lavender and Alan Cavaiola.
     p. cm.
 Includes bibliographical references.
 ISBN 978-1-57224-909-7 (pbk.) -- ISBN 978-1-57224-910-3 (pdf ebook) 1. Narcissism. 2. Interpersonal relations. 3. Interpersonal conflict. I. Cavaiola, Alan A. II. Title.
 BF575.N35.L39 2010
 158.2--dc22

                                    2010043968

12 11 10   10 9 8 7 6 5 4 3 2 1   First printing

We dedicate this book to our wives, a couple of wonderful Irish gals:

To Carolann, for all your love, support, and encouragement.

To Maureen. You are the joy in my life! Thank you for all the ways you love me.

We also dedicate this book to all those who struggle daily in one-way relationships. It's never too late to make changes. May you find peace, serenity, and wholeness in all of your relationships.

Contents

■ Defining Personality Disorders ■ A Growing Trend ■ How This Book Can Help You
■ How to Use This Book

PART 1
Understanding Narcissism and Narcissistic Personality Disorder

CHAPTER 1

■ From Self-Loathing to Healthy Self-Love to Self-Absorbed ■ Defining Narcissism
■ Narcissistic Personality Disorder ■ Personality Disorder vs. Personality Traits ■ Subtypes
or Variations of Narcissistic Personality Disorder ■ Narcissists at Work, Love, and Play
■ How Do Narcissists Get That Way? ■ How the Narcissist Affects You

Acknowledgments

We would like to acknowledge all of our mentors at New Harbinger who have made this workbook possible. We are especially grateful to Jess O'Brien for his patience and support throughout this project and to Jess Beebe for her editorial expertise. You both helped us to communicate clearly and concisely. And a special thanks to Brady Kahn; your suggestions were spot-on. We appreciate all the work you put into this project. We also want to thank the entire New Harbinger staff. You've been wonderful to work with. Also, to those psychologists and researchers who continue to shed light on the evolving topic of personality disorders, we hope and pray that your work will continue to bring healing to those who suffer in loneliness due to lack of knowledge.

We would like to thank our families for their support, especially our lovely wives and golf buddies and our kids, Stephen, Maura, Matthew, Alison, Jay, and Christopher. We are also grateful to our grandchildren for providing comic relief and playtime breaks (when we probably should have been writing or revising). Thank you Tobin, Sophia, and Baby Liam. And Isabelle, Riley, Max, Gavin, and Justin—you guys rock!

Introduction

From the time each of us is a toddler, we are taught that other people's feelings matter, sometimes more than our own. Admonitions such as "You need to share," "You hurt your best friend's feelings," or, more recently, "It's not all about you" are heard by children around the world. It seems that the very act of child rearing is about instructing a child not to be so self-centered and to consider the feelings and needs of those around him. And let's face it: In this life we need others. A lot. Learning to be considerate of others is a prerequisite for a happy and fulfilling life because, after all, we are social creatures designed to live and work with, as well as love, those around us. At the very least, we share a planet together and need to consider the needs of others if we are to survive.

Yet in spite of millions and millions of parents and teachers instructing their children that other people matter—and matter a lot—there are those among us who are incredibly self-centered. They go by different names: Self-absorbed. Pompous. Egocentric. Grandiose. Narcissistic. Expansive and pretentious. Thoughtless and insensitive. Inconsiderate and snobbish. These are only some of the words used to describe people who only care about themselves. These are the people for whom the system just didn't seem to work: selfish little toddlers who, now grown up, never learned that the world doesn't revolve around them.

Worse yet, they really do believe they are special and better than everyone else. Most likely, they will try to set you straight and educate you as to who they really are: they are special, different from everyone else. Indeed, because of this specialness, which makes them better than anyone else, they deserve special treatment. If you are a waitress, they will make sure that you wait only on them to the detriment of all your other customers. If you are their coworker, the no-smoking rule does not apply to them, they will insist, while lighting up and blowing smoke in your face. Such rules were made for others, the mindless sheep who do as they're told. And don't make the mistake of trying to change or correct them—how dare you—by insisting that they be more considerate. They will only try to convince you that the average person is incapable of understanding their brilliance and sheer genius.

Truly, these are an exquisitely self-absorbed and conceited group of people. Psychologists describe them as *narcissistic*, a term that comes from the ancient Greek story of Narcissus, a god so self-centered that he actually fell in love with his own reflection. Narcissism is abnormal and dysfunctional, and it may not surprise you to know that someone who exhibits narcissistic traits may have a real and serious psychological disorder known as *narcissistic personality disorder* (NPD).

The general public has become more familiar with personality disorders like NPD as the number of people with such problems has skyrocketed. Indeed, many experts believe that NPD is reaching pandemic proportions in this country. Why? Perhaps it is the 50 percent divorce rate that leaves children desperately seeking attention and admiration to compensate for feelings of rejection and neglect. Or it is parents all too willing to indulge their kids, assuaging their own guilt by buying them anything they want to atone for their sins of being too busy to spend time with them or to compensate for the divorce. Or perhaps it is the fact that families in the United States are smaller than those around the world and therefore children can demand more. Maybe it is the fact that television promotes an "idols" wannabe mentality—"Wouldn't it be wonderful if all those people were cheering for me?"—followed by a chaser of nonstop advertising promising instant-celebrity status if you only purchase these colognes, jeans, or sneakers.

DEFINING PERSONALITY DISORDERS

Personality disorders are different from other types of psychological disorders. Here, people are not hallucinating, delusional, having panic attacks, or babbling incoherently. They usually do not look or feel mentally ill at all. In fact, they may be the embodiment of what you might call normal: the most popular girl in the class, the teacher everyone adores, or that politician who was going to turn around this economy. But they're not normal.

Personality disorders are a unique group of psychological disorders wherein those afflicted are missing an important part of their personality, such as a conscience or the ability to empathize with others. The rest of their personality appears to be intact, so people with personality disorders may look and act incredibly normal—so normal that it sometimes takes friends and coworkers, even spouses, years to recognize something is wrong. Complicating the diagnosis is the sobering reality that people with personality disorders don't know there is anything wrong with them; they usually blame their problems on others. Although we have seen hundreds of patients in our combined careers and probably hundreds with personality disorders, neither one of us can recall even one person who ever made an appointment to treat his personality disorder. Clients with personality disorders may realize that they have problems in their marriage, with alcoholism, or with another disorder (which may be superimposed on a personality disorder), but not one of our clients has ever recognized his underlying personality disorder. That makes it all the more difficult to deal with.

There are somewhere around eleven to fifteen different types of personality disorders; the number changes according to which expert you are talking to. While each of these disorders is unique, a primary symptom that they all share is the inability to have good interpersonal relationships.

If, among difficult people, those with personality disorders stand out from the crowd, then those people with narcissistic personality disorder stand out even more.

A GROWING TREND

As psychologists, we have seen and treated people with strong narcissistic traits, people with full-blown NPD, and people with other personality disorders, for years, but it wasn't always that way. Whereas earlier in our careers we tended to treat clients with anxiety disorders and various types of depression, more recently we began seeing more and more clients who were having significant problems in their relationships.

Not that relationship issues are anything new. We learned all about relationship issues in graduate school and were subsequently trained in various types of relationship counseling. But what we began seeing in our practices was worlds apart from Mr. and Mrs. Jones learning to adjust to their differences as a married couple or Mr. Smith not getting along with his boss. It seemed that in a growing number of cases, our patients were either narcissistic themselves or they were somehow involved with narcissists: people who were highly toxic and who were causing significant and deep disturbances in the lives of those around them.

We do not use this word "toxic" lightly. These are not simply people who are annoying or a nuisance or just plain-vanilla a pain in the neck. We are referring to people with significant disturbances in the very structure of their personalities, particularly in their ability to relate to others. Indeed, their disturbances in this area may be so powerful that they can actually precipitate problems in the personalities of others. Some therapists refer to such people as "crazy makers" because of their special ability to drive others to the brink of insanity.

Our interest in what we observed led us to conduct a research study and eventually to write a book about toxic coworkers. We surveyed over a thousand people who were working in various occupations and industries, including men and women of different ages who had been on the job for a long time, as well as those who'd been working in their jobs only briefly. And guess what? We found out that it wasn't just our patients who were having problems with others. About 80 percent of the people we surveyed identified as the major source of stress in their job an individual with whom they were having significant and unsettling "issues." For many, it was the number one source of stress in their lives.

These toxic relationships were enormously disturbing. It seemed that each person's tale of woe was worse than the previous one. And the stories we heard! "Oh, you guys are interested in toxic coworkers? Well, I worked with this guy who drove me absolutely crazy. He was always talking about how great he was. If you did something, he would always be the one who did it better. I would stay up all night talking about him and talking about him and talking about him. It drove my wife crazy. 'You just gotta let it go,' she would say. He really got under my skin. I actually had nightmares about him. He practically destroyed me."

These "crazy makers" seemed to consume most of the time, energy, and resources of those surveyed. They were all some people could talk about, even after the research was over. In one instance, we were scheduled to appear on a syndicated radio talk show to talk about different types of toxic coworkers. The producer told us before we went on that the show's host had enjoyed our book in large part because she had been involved with a toxic person and that our book had helped her enormously. The producer further admonished us not to bring up this topic on the show, for it might be embarrassing for the host. Naturally we agreed. But then the host went on to talk for the entire hour about how the narcissist in question had practically ruined her life! We listened as she vented her anger. And that was the entire show. We never even got to speak.

Obviously, we were not the only psychologists who were treating people with relationship issues. As all of this was going on in our professional lives, the whole field of psychology was evolving from the study of what goes on *inside* of people—issues such as anxiety or depression—to what goes on *between* people. Researchers and theoreticians alike were becoming more and more convinced that it is quite possible, for example, for a person to function in a normal manner in all other areas of her life but to have severe deficits in her ability to relate to others. It is surprisingly possible, that is, for someone to be the CEO of a major corporation, making millions of dollars a year, to be the coach of the local football team, and to give thousands of dollars to charity, and to also have a disorder that causes him to function like a three-year-old in his relationships. Not only is it possible, but you see these people all around you. You watch these people regularly on the nightly news. Sometimes they steal millions of dollars from investors. Sometimes they are movie stars who get arrested for beating up their spouses. Sometimes it's the Hollywood couple on their seventeenth divorce. But it is worse yet when you realize that the problem is with your own spouse, child, coworker, or friend.

So somewhere around 1998, we decided to write a book that would address a variety of personality disorders in the workplace. Entitled *Toxic Coworkers* (Cavaiola and Lavender 2000), the book instantly struck a chord with readers. We later conducted seminars across the country for businesses and organizations that had become more interested in identifying and managing this difficult set of people. And without exception, the personality disorder about which they wished to know more than any other was narcissistic personality disorder. People around the world experienced a collective "aha!" experience as they recognized that the secretary who had just taken her nineteenth personal day off, as well as the top salesman who everyone was tired of paying homage to, actually had a bona fide psychological disorder and would most likely never change.

But we realized that narcissistic people are not limited to the workplace. They can be found most anywhere: They may be your mother or sister, father or brother, spouse or child. They may be your coworker, friend, teammate, or teacher. Therefore, we decided to write this book for anyone who is involved with a self-centered narcissistic person, whether that person is your coworker, friend, lover, or family member.

HOW THIS BOOK CAN HELP YOU

You might ask, why didn't we choose to write a book that would help people who have narcissistic personality disorder? The short answer is that it wouldn't sell. One of the key symptoms of this disorder is that people are unaware that they have it. Actually, if you were to tell someone that she had narcissistic personality disorder, she would most likely answer, "Well, I am special. I am uniquely gifted and talented. I am far too complex for the average psychologist to understand. That doesn't make it a disorder, does it?" In fact, while we have never had anyone ask us to be treated for narcissism, our practices are filled with people whom the self-centered have wounded in some way.

So, is this book for you?

It is our firm belief that having regular contact with a self-absorbed, self-centered, narcissistic person, who cares little about you and who uses you for his own self-inflation, is one of the hardest things you can experience in life. It can sap you of your energy, keep you up at night, break up your family, destroy a friendship, or make for a dysfunctional workplace. Unbeknownst to many people who are involved in difficult relationships is the fact that they are tangling with someone who has strong narcissistic traits or even narcissistic personality disorder. Note: Throughout this book we use the word "narcissism" or "narcissist" to describe people who exhibit strong narcissistic traits, even if they are not diagnosable with NPD. This book is designed to help you if you are involved with someone who meets this description.

If you purchased this book, it is most likely that you are involved in a one-way relationship. Perhaps you are tired of playing second fiddle to your spouse, with his constant demands for you to put his needs first, support his wild and grandiose pipe dreams, and make him look good in front of others. Perhaps you work for a narcissist and you have become sick and tired of her lack of responsiveness to your requests and her insistence that you do things outside the scope of your job description. Perhaps it is your coworker who continuously steals your ideas, basking in the glory that should have been yours, and then has the nerve to tell you that you need to work harder. Perhaps you have a narcissistic friend who must be in the limelight constantly, who never gives you credit for anything that goes well in your life, and who constantly brags about all of his accomplishments, especially when holding court in the company of others. Perhaps you're involved with a sibling who sucks your family's resources dry as she demands constant and exclusive attention to whatever cause of the day she happens to be championing. Maybe it's a parent who was so self-absorbed that you never received the nurturing that you needed as you were growing up.

If any of these situations sounds familiar, you are in the right place.

HOW TO USE THIS BOOK

We wanted to make a workbook that would not only inform our readers but also transform their relationships. So we designed this book with that purpose always in the forefront. This format is carefully designed to take you step-by-step through the labyrinth of dysfunctional narcissistic relationship patterns until they are finally changed.

We have structured this book in the following manner: In part 1, we talk about the various signs and symptoms of narcissism. Here we discuss a spectrum of self-centeredness ranging from moderate self-absorption all the way to full-blown narcissistic personality disorder. While no two narcissists are the same, they do share common characteristics, and we describe each symptom, one by one. Perhaps more importantly, we talk about how these symptoms can affect you and can actually get you to feel, think, and behave differently than you do around others. Knowing the symptoms of NPD helps you to recognize them and to manage more effectively when you are with the narcissist. It will also validate many of the feelings you have had about your narcissistic relationship, things you might have felt weren't quite right but were not really sure of. As you examine the vast array of highly disturbing feelings these self-absorbed individuals can bring out in you, you will understand better why this relationship has been so difficult for you. Part 1 also covers different narcissistic subtypes, for, yes, narcissistic people come in many forms and some of them initially don't seem narcissistic it all. We want to make you aware of all these types, so they don't fly under your radar.

Part 2 gives you practical strategies for managing the unique narcissist in your life and making your situation a lot healthier. Let's face it: The narcissist is a formidable adversary indeed, and if you are involved with one, you have struck the mother lode of dysfunction. Better to be prepared! You need to be equipped with special skills to deal with the narcissist. Part 2 gives you plenty of practice in applying what you learn from this book, and the exercises should more than adequately prepare you to effectively manage the narcissist's unrelenting selfishness.

Be aware that some of these exercises can become challenging. Going beyond just preparing you to cope, they help you to master and transform your situation. Be ready to grow and stretch yourself beyond what you are used to. After mastering these concepts, you will be able to free yourself from the bonds of narcissistic relationships throughout your life, and although an occasional narcissist might get the better of you, you'll be way ahead of the average Joe who is enmeshed in a quagmire of dysfunction with yet another self-absorbed individual.

Study and work hard. We wish you all the best in transforming your relationships!

Understanding Narcissism and Narcissistic Personality Disorder

The Narcissistic Personality

Living or working with someone who is narcissistic can be very frustrating and at times very distressing. If you're in a relationship with a narcissist, you may often find yourself asking, "When will it ever be about me?" You may eventually come to realize that you will never be a priority in the life of your self-absorbed other. This is a hard realization to come to, but what keeps people locked into their narcissistic other is the hope that someday the person will snap out of it or come around to truly being able to love others. Isn't that what we all want: to feel connection with others, to love and be loved? For narcissists, somehow this need for connection and love gets obscured.

This chapter will look at the entire range of narcissistic personality issues, from mild narcissistic personality traits to the full-blown personality disorder. It will help you determine whether the person in your life is, in fact, a narcissist.

FROM SELF-LOATHING TO HEALTHY SELF-LOVE TO NARCISSISM

In discussing narcissism, it is helpful to think of a person's feelings about himself as being on a continuum (see the illustration on the next page). At one end of the continuum is self-loathing, or self-hatred. We all know people like this. They are extremely self-critical, and if you give them a compliment, they will come up with a way to downplay it. This personality trait is much the opposite of narcissism. In the middle of the continuum is healthy self-love. This can best be described as occurring when people value themselves, they take care of themselves, and they can stick up for themselves. A person who embraces healthy self-love is able to love others because she is confident in herself and therefore can express love without fear of being hurt or rejected. People who epitomize healthy self-love are likely to engage in altruistic behaviors. Such was the case with Dr. Jonas Salk, the pathologist who discovered the polio vaccine. Although Dr. Salk could have sold the vaccine to a pharmaceutical company for millions, he made his discovery available to everyone so that he could better prevent human suffering. This is truly exemplary of someone who manifests healthy self-love, also known as a self-actualized person (Maslow 1970).

Narcissism falls at the other end of the continuum and is characterized by people who are so self-absorbed and caught up in their own agenda that they can't really see other people or their needs. As with the mythical Narcissus, they are caught up in their own reflection and image. Therefore, they are incapable of loving others and can only love themselves.

The Self-Love Continuum

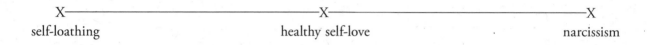

X————————————————————————X————————————————————————X
self-loathing   healthy self-love   narcissism

DEFINING NARCISSISM

Let's start with a practical definition of narcissism. Narcissists are people who feel that they are special or unique and therefore deserve to be treated as special by others. They often have grandiose and arrogant attitudes in their interactions with others and expect others to see their unique talents and abilities. Narcissists are generally unhappy unless they are receiving accolades and tributes from those around them. They tend to lack empathy and have a limited capacity to love. Narcissists often have fantasies of unlimited power, brilliance, or wealth. They tend to exploit others to their own ends and be distrustful of others.

In looking at this definition, you can see why it is very difficult to live with, be in a relationship with, or work with someone who has narcissistic personality disorder or has deeply ingrained narcissistic traits. Here are two examples of people who exhibit narcissist traits.

◆ Alex, the Stockbroker

Alex is twenty-eight years old and is a stockbroker with a major investment firm in the city. He received his MBA from a prestigious business school, graduating at the top of his class, and he does not miss an opportunity to let anyone and everyone know about it. He drives an expensive sports car, belongs to the most exclusive country club, and eats at the best restaurants. Alex feels that he deserves only the best because he is incredibly talented and special. Although Alex is considered a top producer at his job, he is not well liked, nor does he show much loyalty to the corporation he works for. Alex's boss resents that he is never on time for work and that Alex thinks nothing of making demeaning remarks about his management style. Alex went behind his boss's back to see if he could get a promotion. Alex's coworkers also see him as being Machiavellian and a cutthroat, someone who would "throw his own mother under the bus" in order to get ahead. When it comes to work, Alex basically feels that the rules don't apply to him. He is abusive to the administrative assistants and has been known to make sexually offensive remarks. Some of the women who work in his department have considered filing a complaint against

Alex. His administrative assistant says the only time Alex is nice to her is when he needs something done fast or he needs her to cover for one of his careless mistakes. Alex's attitude toward women is also reflected in his dating habits. He generally does not date a woman for more than a couple of months because he doesn't want to "get tied down."

Now let's look at someone else who manifests many narcissistic traits. See if you can pick up on some essential differences between Alex and Debbie as you read about her.

◆ *Debbie, the Self-Absorbed Parent*

Debbie's ex-husband once remarked that a cat is a better mother to her kittens than Debbie is to her kids. He was amazed at how she never wanted to attend their daughter's soccer games on Saturday mornings because she didn't want to miss an appointment to have her nails done. When Bob divorced Debbie, it was because she refused to do anything together with the family. Debbie preferred to go out with her single friends and would never miss a fashion show at the club. It seemed that the only time Debbie would pay attention to her daughter and son was when she was required to because all the other mothers would be there (such as school plays or other events). Debbie once sent her son to school when he was running a fever because she didn't want to miss her exercise class. When the school nurse called Debbie to have her pick up her son, Debbie launched into a tirade and threatened to sue the nurse for "malpractice." Debbie is accustomed to getting her own way and will often use threats or intimidation to do so.

Both Alex and Debbie have extreme narcissistic traits. Notice how their self-centeredness permeates just about every aspect of their lives, whether it be romantic relationships, friendships, jobs, or family life. It is not unusual for narcissists to go through a string of relationships, friendships, or marriages because no one is ever good enough for them.

NARCISSISTIC PERSONALITY DISORDER

So, what does it mean to say that a person has narcissistic personality disorder? Generally, this disorder refers to a pervasive maladaptive pattern characterized by grandiose attitudes and behavior, an excessive need for admiration, and a lack of empathy. People with narcissistic personality disorder generally tend to think of themselves as being special and unique. They are quite skilled at exaggerating their own accomplishments or self-aggrandizing, and they often come across to others as being boastful and pretentious. People with this disorder are also quite envious of others and will begrudge others their successes, accomplishments, or possessions. Given their lack of empathy, people with NPD often become impatient with others, especially when it comes to dealing with their problems or frailties. It may also be difficult for someone with NPD to recognize others' needs and to be genuinely concerned with their welfare.

To be diagnosed with narcissistic personality disorder, people must exhibit at least five of the following symptoms (American Psychiatric Association 2000):

1. having a grandiose sense of self-importance (exaggerating achievements)

2. having a preoccupation with fantasies of unlimited success, power, brilliance, and so on

3. believing that they are special or unique and therefore can only be understood by other special or unique or high-status people

4. having an excessive need for admiration

5. having a sense of entitlement

6. exploiting others for personal gain or benefit

7. lacking the ability to empathize with others

8. envying others and believing that others are envious of them

9. being very arrogant and haughty

Now let's go back and look at Alex and Debbie and see how they compare to the diagnostic criteria. Alex clearly displays five symptoms of narcissistic personality disorder. For example, his grandiose sense of self-importance is evident in how he flaunts his MBA from a prestigious business school. His self-perception that he is special or unique and therefore can only be understood by those of similar stature is evident in Alex's view that he deserves the best because he is uniquely talented. His sense of entitlement shows up in many areas: going behind his boss's back for a raise, coming in late for work, and making demeaning remarks to women coworkers. All illustrate Alex's perception that the usual rules don't apply to him. His exploitation of others is also evident in how he treats his boss, his coworkers, the administrative staff, and the women he dates. Alex is clearly the type of person who steps on others to get ahead or to get his own needs met. It is not uncommon that people like this will also lack empathy for others because they lack the ability to see things from someone else's perspective. Finally, Alex's arrogance and haughty behavior are evident in how he interacts with others and flaunts his achievements and accomplishments. Alex meets the criteria for narcissistic personality disorder.

Debbie has many narcissistic qualities, but even though her narcissistic traits are in some ways more severe than Alex's, it's more difficult to diagnose her definitively with narcissistic personality disorder. For example, while Alex tends to exploit everyone with whom he comes in contact, Debbie seems to confine her exploitation of others to her immediate family. Similarly, whereas Alex is adept at flaunting his grandiose sense of self-importance (which relates to his display of arrogance or haughty behavior), Debbie is personally self-absorbed but not so intent on impressing others with her achievements. Debbie does display a sense of entitlement; just ask any of the teachers at her children's school or the school nurse whom she threatened to sue. So while Debbie has many narcissistic traits, she does not appear to neatly fit the criteria for narcissistic personality disorder, and to properly diagnose her, a professional would need to see if her beliefs and attitudes reflect the extreme self-centeredness that is so typical of those with NPD. (Warning: In describing the symptoms of narcissistic personality disorder, our goal is not to turn you into a diagnostician or mental health professional but rather to acquaint you with some of the symptoms and problems that are common to those with NPD and to help you determine if these traits, attitudes, beliefs, and behaviors are similar to what you may be encountering.)

Throughout this workbook, you will find examples of both men and women with narcissistic personality disorder and narcissistic traits. It should be noted, however, that 50 to 75 percent of all people diagnosed with NPD are male and that NPD occurs in anywhere from 2 to 16 percent of the adult American population (American Psychiatric Association 2000).

PERSONALITY DISORDER VS. PERSONALITY TRAITS

It is quite possible for a person to exhibit some narcissistic traits but not necessarily manifest the full-blown personality disorder. One of the key distinctions here is that people with NPD often display narcissistic traits or characteristics that are both pervasive and maladaptive.

So, is the person in your life a narcissist? You can begin to answer this question by taking an inventory of his or her narcissistic traits.

Exercise: You May Be Dealing with a Narcissist If...

Place a checkmark next to any of the following narcissistic traits that would apply to the person you know.

- ☐ It's always about him or her, never about you.

- ☐ His or her needs or desires always come before yours.

- ☐ He or she is good at making you feel inferior.

- ☐ You often feel exploited or used by him or her.

- ☐ He or she demands your admiration and constant attention.

- ☐ He or she is often grandiose and acts in an arrogant, haughty manner.

- ☐ He or she lacks empathy and has trouble expressing loving feelings.

- ☐ He or she is good at charming people or selling people on his or her ideas.

- ☐ He or she often wants to be in a position of power or to have control over others.

- ☐ He or she feels that the rules don't apply in his or her case.

- ☐ He or she is preoccupied with fantasies of wealth and fame.

- ☐ He or she is seen as a blowhard by friends or relatives.

Chances are if you checked three or more of the above traits, you may be dealing with someone with narcissistic personality traits or narcissistic personality disorder.

It is easy to get sucked in by a narcissist's wit, charm, or charisma. He will often have quite a knack for winning people over or selling them on his ideas. It is no wonder, then, that narcissists are attracted to positions of power or to relationships in which they have the upper hand, yet they also want to be around others whom they perceive as complementing their own attractiveness. Remember, however, that in any relationship, narcissists are only out for themselves or what they think they can get out of the relationship, not what they can give to the relationship.

SUBTYPES OR VARIATIONS OF NARCISSISTIC PERSONALITY DISORDER

Not all narcissists are the same. Psychologist Theodore Millon (1996) described the following subtypes of people with NPD: the unprincipled narcissist, the amorous narcissist, the compensatory narcissist, and the elitist narcissist. As you read about these subtypes, see if any seem similar to the person you have concerns about. Note that both men and women can fall into any of these categories, and the narcissist in your life may exhibit traits of more than one subtype.

The Unprincipled Narcissist

What characterizes unprincipled narcissists is that they seem to be devoid of a conscience, or sense of right and wrong. They are often unconcerned with the welfare of others and are amoral, unscrupulous, and deceptive in their dealings with others. They exude an arrogant sense of self-worth and grandiosity. They are driven by a need to outwit others, which proves that they are smarter than those they prey on. It's not unusual to find this type of narcissist in jails, prisons, and drug rehabilitation centers, although many unprincipled narcissists go through life without running afoul of the law.

The Amorous Narcissist

Amorous narcissists have an erotic or seductive orientation. They construct and measure their self-worth around sexual conquests. They often run through a string of pathological relationships, casting aside the person they have just seduced only to look for their next conquest. Amorous narcissists are often known for being heartbreakers, as well as committing some rather outrageous acts, such as conning their sexual partners out of huge sums of money, pathological lying, and other types of fraudulent behavior. The amorous narcissist is truly the Don Juan character who compensates for deeper feelings of inadequacy by seducing others and taking them for all they're worth. Each sexual conquest reinforces the amorous narcissist's sense of self-worth and overinflated self-image.

The Compensatory Narcissist

The compensatory narcissist is driven by a need to compensate for past hurts or childhood emotional wounds by creating an illusion of superiority. Compensatory narcissists live in a fantasy world of their own creation in which they "pursue the leading role in a false and imaginary theater" (Millon 1996, 411) rather than living their own lives. They are driven to enhance their self-esteem through what are often imagined achievements. In order to achieve this goal of prestige, compensatory narcissists need an audience of others who will buy into their deception. In fact, compensatory narcissists are often hypervigilant or highly sensitive to how others react to or perceive them, often watching or carefully listening for any signs of criticism or disdain.

The Elitist Narcissist

In some ways similar to compensatory narcissists, elitist narcissists are often obsessed with their own inflated self-image. They often create a false sense of self that bears little resemblance to their actual self, yet they manage to convince themselves (and often those around them) of their unique talents and abilities. They feel empowered and entitled to special treatment because of whatever status or pseudo-achievements they may have attained. Elitist narcissists often turn relationships into competitions or contests, whether they are work relationships, friendships, or even love relationships. Here the goal is winning, no matter what the means or cost, in order to prove to others (and themselves) their incomparable superiority. Elitist narcissists are often social climbers and they think nothing of stepping on or over anyone in their quest for fame and status. They are very adept at marketing themselves and will not shrink from any opportunity to do so. Because elitist narcissists hold themselves in such high regard, they see little need to listen to others or follow directions.

Other Narcissistic Subtypes

In our work with clients, students, and various corporations, we see quite a bit of entitlement and narcissistic behavior, and we've developed our own list of more contemporary subtypes that seem to fit with the times. As you read about our subtypes, which follow, do any seem similar to the narcissist in your life?

The trust fund baby: Somewhat similar to Theodore Millon's elitist narcissist (1996), trust fund babies are narcissists who grew up with the proverbial silver spoon in their mouth and have no hesitancy about letting others know of their pedigree, their financial worth, what exclusive prep school they went to, and so on. What's often very interesting about these narcissists is that they grew up feeling special and therefore entitled. As a result, they often have little capacity for empathy and little time or interest in anyone whom they perceive to be of lower social status. When it comes to the personal troubles of others, as Marie

Antoinette put it, "Let them eat cake!" Naturally, not everyone born to wealth and privilege becomes a narcissist; there are those who do incredibly philanthropic work and aspire to professions in which they do good works on behalf of others.

The profession-bound narcissist: There are narcissists whose entire identity is tied up in who they are as professionals. Whether they are doctors, lawyers, judges, financial experts, musicians, actors, or academics, their egos are so enormous that they need a tractor-trailer to haul them around. These are the people who like to flaunt their power and in doing so are often abusive to anyone who crosses their path or gets in their way. You'll see these folks driving around in the latest sports car with vanity license plates, as if announcing to the world what they do for a living. Think of it this way: when someone is truly at the top of his field, does he really need to flaunt it?

The child prodigy narcissist: Some people believe they are unique and special because they grew up with a lot of adults constantly reminding them that they were. From the star athlete to the gifted musician to the most gifted student, they received more than their share of the glory and accolades while growing up. Unfortunately, this early fame seems to go to their heads, as they too begin to feel that they are larger than life. We hear many stories of child stars and prodigies who end up having miserable adult lives that are marred by drug or alcohol addiction and emotional turmoil. Just being average or being a face in the crowd is not okay for these narcissists, who need to be recognized and the center of attention wherever they go. It's no wonder that former child prodigies often cannot stand the fact that they no longer have special status. We often see them in the university setting: having come through gifted and talented programs throughout grammar school and high school, these former child prodigies often conclude that their talents will carry them through college-level courses without needing to put in the work to obtain an A. They often feel they should be given an A because they're entitled to it.

The closet narcissist: Probably the most difficult to discern, closet narcissists often appear on the surface to be just like everyone else. It's not until you get to know them or you scratch beneath the surface that you begin to see their true selves. When this happens, you begin to see their arrogance, haughtiness, and expectation to be treated as special, or their need to exert power over others. What makes these narcissists difficult to identify is that they often seek out professions or positions in which you ordinarily wouldn't expect to find narcissists, such as in human services, in teaching, or even among the clergy. What becomes obvious after a period of time, however, is that they are not about helping others but about self-aggrandizement. They are not about helping those whom they are supposed to serve but about building their own egos up (at others' expense).

The know-it-all narcissist: This subtype resembles the profession-bound narcissist, but you may find this type of narcissist in almost any walk of life. Often these know-it-alls lack a complete education, but they go through life browbeating others into coming around to their way of thinking. They usually have very definite opinions about nearly everything, and they feel they have been put on this earth to offer up their little pearls of wisdom on whatever unsuspecting victim happens to give them an ear. Know-it-alls can be expected to be right about everything—remember the cardinal rule "Don't confuse them with the facts," because their minds are made up and they will be unrelenting until they have changed your mind as well. Sometimes it's best just to let them rant and rave and to go on your merry way. If you are a captive audience, however, hopefully your patience will hold up.

The addicted narcissist: One of the unfortunate by-products of addiction (whether it be to drugs, alcohol, sex, gambling, or shopping) is that addicts become incapable of loving others. One sure sign of addiction is that an addict will consistently put a drug of choice over loved ones. It goes with the territory, which is why addicts will think nothing of stealing from their families, lying, or conning them. This type of behavior can be seen as a form of narcissism, albeit drug-induced but a narcissistic process nevertheless. Fortunately, one of the miraculous changes that occurs when someone truly embraces recovery (and begins to work a structured, consistent recovery program) is that you begin to see a transformation from a narcissistic or egocentric way of life to one in which the now recovering person can love others and participate fully in loving relationships. Unfortunately, we have also seen instances where people claim to be recovering but remain as self-centered as they were when they were actively addicted. Usually this lack of change or growth can be traced back to something lacking in the way they've worked their recovery program.

Exercise: Narcissist Subtypes

Does the narcissist in your life match one of these subtypes? Is he or she a combination of types? In the space below, please write about how the person in your life matches any of the subtypes we've described.

_____

_____

_____

If the person in your life doesn't fit any of these descriptions, remember that these subtypes are merely guidelines; narcissism is not defined by them.

NARCISSISTS AT WORK, LOVE, AND PLAY

You may find that the narcissist in your life is your boss, coworker, or subordinate; your spouse or partner; or your friend. This is not to imply that there are narcissists lurking under every bush or around every corner just waiting to pounce, but it is not unusual to find narcissists in many different types of relationships.

The Narcissist at Work

Narcissists are often attracted to positions of power and prestige. Therefore, it's not unusual to find narcissists in professions such as law or medicine, or as CEOs of companies, stockbrokers, military officers, professors, or even clergy members. Given these positions, however, it is also not uncommon for narcissists to abuse that power, which is why you're likely to find narcissists being overrepresented among workplace bullies and those accused of sexual harassment or creating a hostile work environment. When working for a narcissistic boss or administrator, you're likely to encounter the following:

- They exploit those who work for them.

- They may steal your work and claim it as their own.

- Their lack of empathy will be reflected in their lack of concern for any personal problems or difficulties you may experience.

- Narcissists are not good mentors or teachers; they will expect you to read their mind or know what they want without directly communicating it.

- They will think nothing of making demeaning or derogatory comments or telling an offensive joke.

- They will expect you to put in endless hours of work or to sacrifice family time when they don't.

- They will not miss any opportunity to promote themselves, and they will expect you to promote them as well.

- They are disloyal and will sell out even their most trusted employee in a flash.

If you've had the misfortune of working for a narcissistic boss or administrator, then most of these behaviors will seem all too familiar to you.

Administrators and bosses are not the only narcissists, however. You may be working with a narcissistic employee, for example, someone who is basically incapable of loyalty because he is only loyal to himself. Some managers and administrators we've counseled say that having a narcissistic subordinate is like having a poisonous snake running loose in your house, never knowing where it's lurking or when it's going to strike.

Finally, the narcissist in your life may be a coworker or colleague. The advantage here is that power is probably not an issue in your relationship. But it is never easy having a narcissist in the workplace, no matter who she may be. This workbook will help you reduce your stress level whether the narcissist in your work life is a boss, employee, or coworker.

The Narcissist in Love

Being involved in a love relationship with a narcissist can be frustrating. Some contend that it is difficult, if not impossible, to be involved in a true love relationship with a narcissist because the narcissist is only in love with herself. Although you may sometimes hope for an equal partnership, it never seems to happen. Because narcissists don't wear signs saying "Beware: I am only capable of loving myself," it's very common for people to find themselves in love with someone whose narcissistic personality traits don't surface until well into the relationship.

Early on, it may be difficult to tell. Narcissists are often quite charming and very skilled at what is called impression management. Some are keenly aware of how to read people and respond accordingly. Over time, however, narcissists begin to show their true colors. A client once remarked that she first became aware of her fiancé's narcissistic streak when he refused to accompany her to the funeral of her favorite aunt because he had made plans to play golf with a business associate. Another client said he only became fully aware of his wife's narcissistic tendencies when she refused to pick him up from the hospital after minor surgery because she had an appointment with her masseuse. These may seem like minor examples of self-centeredness, but for each of these clients, they represented a moment of insight into their partner's narcissism, especially since these incidents resembled so many prior instances of similar behavior.

It's common for people to be blind to their partner's narcissism, given the narcissist's ability to create a favorable first impression. Partners of narcissists will often comment on the narcissist's many admirable qualities, such as his confidence or her sense of humor or how good he is as a financial provider. However, in the overall scope of the relationship, partners of narcissists often feel that something is lacking, and although it may be hard at first to discern exactly what that something is, it usually becomes apparent over time. Partners often find themselves initially being irritated or angry in social situations when the narcissistic spouse or partner always steers the conversation toward one of his accomplishments or conquests; they discover that the narcissistic partner needs to be the center of attention, no matter what the occasion.

The Narcissist as a Friend

As with love relationships, extreme self-centeredness is a problem in friendships with narcissists. You may find that you are always there for your narcissistic friend, but somehow she is never really there for you. Or you may find yourself always doing what he wants and on his time schedule, but somehow you never get around to doing things that you want to do or at your convenience. Being the best friend of a narcissist is not an easy task; however, in a friendship you have a better chance of limiting your contact. In a love relationship or in a work setting, you may be a captive audience to the narcissist's exquisite game, which is often designed to exploit you and to aggrandize the narcissist. Later in this workbook, we will help you look more closely at relationships with narcissists in your social and love life and will offer some strategies for how best to manage your relationships in these spheres.

HOW DO NARCISSISTS GET THAT WAY?

With all the talk about the influences of genetics and neurotransmitters on behavior, you may wonder if there is some genetic link to narcissistic personality disorder or some chemical imbalance that causes it. Unfortunately, although it's tempting to draw such a conclusion, it's more likely that narcissists are not born that way but develop narcissistic traits. Indeed, there are many theories for how narcissism develops, but going into all of them is beyond the scope of this workbook. The two theories presented here are among the most popular and compelling. One of these theories is that people develop narcissistic traits in response to how they were parented. The other theory is that these traits evolve out of deep-seated feelings of inferiority.

Parenting Style

Most adolescents are indeed self-centered and narcissistic. It seems to go with the territory of being a teenager. Teens have a unique talent for seeing life through only their own eyes of teenage angst. This is one of the reasons why teenagers can be so cruel and bullying to their peers or parents. However, most people who survive adolescence are able to shed their egocentric views and begin to develop a sense of empathy for others, especially as they begin to develop the capacity to look at things from different perspectives.

If you have a teenage child who is very self-centered, you may very well ask whether this means she will grow up to become a narcissist. The answer is probably not. One reason that teenagers are never diagnosed with personality disorders is that their personalities are still developing. As a parent, you can encourage your egocentric teenager to put herself in the other person's shoes or to look at things from other perspectives. This may help her develop empathy. Some teenagers are naturally more empathic, and seeing things from another's point of view comes to them more easily. For others, empathy takes some time to develop, especially if they've been accustomed to having things go their way or they've received a lot of attention or accolades.

It seems that those who go on to become full-fledged narcissists, however, may have experienced a parenting style that was either overindulgent and pampering or neglectful and rejecting. Freud (1914) was one of the early theorists to describe this type of parenting style. Some narcissistic personalities were parented in such a way as to convey that they were the center of the universe. This is true of "stage mothers" and "coach fathers" who teach their kids that the world should and does revolve around them. This may also occur in child-centered families in which the marital bond is rather weak or nonexistent; it is easier for these couples to focus their lives around their child.

In the opposite scenario, where parents are neglectful, rejecting, or sometimes fickle or erratic, children learn that they cannot depend on their parents for nurturance or love. These children essentially give up trusting that their parents will love them and basically turn to the only person they feel they can trust: themselves. This shift toward self-love is seen as an attempt at self-preservation.

Compensating for Feelings of Inferiority

Another theory that helps to explain why some people become narcissists and others don't is found in the theory of compensation (Reich 1960). This theory is that narcissism is rooted in feelings of inferiority; to overcome these feelings, the narcissist adopts a pattern of behavior in which he overcompensates by overachieving. Akhtar and Thomson (1982) explain that although people with NPD appear grandiose, seductive, and exploitative, they are actually doubt-ridden, chronically bored, envious of others' achievements, and unable to love. Their overcompensation is often played out in such arenas as occupational endeavors, financial success, or having the most attractive mate. We've all seen people who overcompensate by purchasing the fanciest cars, the largest or fastest boats, or the most luxurious penthouse condo. It is as if they were saying, "Look at me; see how successful I am." The old joke "the bigger the car, the smaller the penis" may not be that far from the truth. It may indeed be a feeling of smallness, or inferiority, that causes some narcissists to behave the way they do.

It may seem contradictory that those who harbor feelings of inferiority would want to draw attention to themselves, but the theory is that in doing so, they are trying to gain the admiration of other people. Narcissists may perceive themselves as lovable based upon their ability to get others to love them, and they therefore feel compelled to draw attention to themselves so that others will see just how lovable and admirable they are. Think about the Michael Scott character on the popular TV series *The Office*. Michael is the epitome of the narcissistic boss, constantly trying to draw attention to himself no matter how inappropriate it may be. He is always seeking the attention and admiration of his staff. Not surprisingly, some episodes of this series describe Michael as having been a rejected loner as a child, an extremely awkward and geekish adolescent. He is an excellent example of an overcompensating, overachieving narcissistic adult. He is unable to show any empathy toward others, which often results in his making inappropriate, boorish comments.

HOW THE NARCISSIST AFFECTS YOU

Throughout this workbook, you'll be asked to look at how you react to the narcissist in your life as a way of focusing on areas that you'd like to change. Here is an exercise to get started.

Exercise: How Does the Narcissist Affect Your Feelings?

It is common when dealing with a narcissist in either your personal or work life to be frustrated, angry, and disappointed. Respond to the following statements on a scale of 1 to 4, where 1 means you strongly disagree, 2 means you disagree, 3 means you agree, and 4 means you strongly agree.

_____ 1. You often feel like you're second fiddle to his or her desires or wants.

_____ 2. You feel angry that he or she is not more caring or loving.

_____ 3. You often expect him or her to act differently and feel disappointed when this doesn't happen.

_____ 4. You often feel left out of his or her life or plans.

_____ 5. You feel exploited or used by him or her.

_____ 6. You often feel that you would be better off on your own.

_____ 7. You admire his or her self-confidence.

_____ 8. You're often struck by his or her ability to charm people or win them over.

_____ 9. He or she puts you down or criticizes you a lot, which makes you feel hurt or angry.

_____ 10. He or she thinks nothing of making decisions without you, which makes you feel invisible and left out.

_____ 11. He or she always wants your undivided attention and admiration, and you find yourself feeling drained or exhausted by the constant demands.

_____ 12. He or she often invalidates or ignores your feelings.

_____ 13. His or her need to be the center of attention often embarrasses you.

Now add up the score. If you scored between 45 and 52, you probably have a lot of intense feelings toward the narcissist in your life. If you scored between 30 and 44, you're probably coping with the narcissist but have times when you may feel intense anger, hurt, or disappointment. If you scored lower than 30, you probably don't allow the narcissist to impact your reactions very often.

Chapter 2 will expand on some of the topics presented in this chapter and will provide you with some strategies for both identifying NPD and narcissistic traits and managing your life with your narcissistic coworker, lover, family member, or friend.

Are You Dealing with a Narcissist?

You may be asking the question "Is the person in my life really a narcissist?" This chapter will help you answer that question more definitively by taking a closer look at the other person's behaviors and their effect on you.

This chapter will give you a fresh understanding of your history with this person, enabling you to interpret problematic interactions in a new way. You should find this not only enlightening but also useful as you begin to construct better coping strategies.

Being able to accurately define your difficulties with the other person is the beginning of a real solution. In the past, it may have seemed that you were going from one confusing and entangled interaction to another, leaving you hurt and bewildered. Now you will be able to recognize the other person's strategies so clearly that they will stand out like flashing neon signs pointing the way toward a much more effective response from you.

THE NARCISSIST CHANGES THE WAY YOU THINK, FEEL, AND ACT

Narcissists will make you think differently, feel differently, and act differently than you do with anyone else. Narcissists affect you in a much deeper and more pervasive way than do other simply "difficult" people. There are people whom you simply may not like for one reason or another, but, for the most part, when you deal with them, you are very much yourself. When you are with someone who has narcissistic traits, however, it's almost like you develop another personality, one that you do not like very much. Whereas previously you might have been outgoing and sociable, around the narcissist you feel withdrawn and shy. Usually when you are around others, you feel that your opinions are intelligent and well thought out, but when you're involved in an interaction with a narcissist, you feel that what you have to say is stupid and insignificant. If you are usually well-spoken, you will stutter. If you are good at your job, you will be a bungler around the narcissist. You are simply not yourself and most likely are upset with yourself because you cannot be yourself when you are around this person.

Some psychologists refer to this process as *projective identification*. A simple way to describe this rather complex behavioral interaction is that the narcissist somehow makes you assume a role that will meet her needs. For example, if a narcissist needs to argue or have a debate with someone, you will find yourself suddenly wanting to argue and debate. This will hold true even if you are usually not the type of person who likes to argue. If a narcissist needs to seduce others, you might find yourself sexually attracted to him, even if you are really not looking for a sexual partner. We know that sounds strange, but it's true. It almost feels like a magic spell has been cast on you that utterly transforms you.

Another way to tell you are involved with a narcissist is that the other person seems to occupy all your thoughts all of the time. This can be incredibly odd. You just can't help it. You find yourself fixated on the other person. A different way of putting this is that the narcissist lives in your brain rent free. You find yourself wanting to think about other things, but you can't. Not only will you continually think about the narcissist, but you will find this person entering into your conversations in the strangest of ways. You will be talking about the new car you are considering buying one minute, and the next minute you'll be talking about your narcissistic brother who never does his share around the holidays. Go figure. You'll probably even find yourself dreaming about the narcissist. An accounting professor who had a narcissistic mother would visit his mother, who lived alone, and then return to his wife and home, only to complain all night long about his mother's arrogance and grandiosity. This went on until finally one night his wife gave him an ultimatum: to never talk about his mother again or to confront the end of his marriage.

The following exercises will take a closer look at how the narcissistic person in your life affects your feelings, actions, and thoughts.

Exercise: How Do You React to the Narcissistic Person in Your Life?

Place a checkmark next to any of the following ways that you react or change around the narcissistic person in your life.

☐ differently from how you feel with other people

☐ used

☐ stupid for being involved with him or her

☐ inferior

☐ humiliated

☐ like your only worth is as a cheerleader or fan

- ☐ frustrated that you can never get a word in edgewise
- ☐ insignificant, just an annoyance to him or her
- ☐ inadequate
- ☐ needy because it seems like you need this person more than he or she needs you
- ☐ like you're a big sucker
- ☐ fearful for your safety
- ☐ manipulated
- ☐ unimportant because your feelings just don't matter
- ☐ afraid of abandonment
- ☐ cheated because everything seems to be about his or her needs
- ☐ ignored or invisible because your opinions seem unimportant to him or her
- ☐ apprehensive of quick retaliation if you do anything to upset him or her
- ☐ frustrated because you're forced to listen to him or her bragging
- ☐ unhappy that the relationship is less important to him or her than to you
- ☐ insignificant as you're always in his or her shadow
- ☐ insecure because you don't ever know whether he or she is going to reject or love you
- ☐ victimized, taken advantage of
- ☐ nervous, like you are walking on eggshells or afraid you will do something wrong
- ☐ overburdened as he or she never pulls his or her own weight
- ☐ dominated as he or she talks at you, not with you
- ☐ angry to the point of wanting to hurt this person in some way

List some other ways that your behavior or emotions change around this person:

_____

_____

_____

_____

Besides affecting how you feel, a narcissist can also have an impact on how you behave. The next exercise helps you examine how this person changes your behavior.

Exercise: How Does Your Behavior Change Around the Narcissist?

Place a checkmark next to the following ways that you act or have acted in response to this person that seem different from the way you would usually act. With this person, you do the following:

☐ avoid confrontations

☐ avoid important discussions that may result in you being personally attacked or put down

☐ subjugate your own needs

☐ pull more than your own weight

☐ chase the person to bring him or her back into the relationship

☐ continually reassure the other person about how great he or she is

☐ use alcohol or drugs to cope with this relationship

☐ have disturbing dreams about the other person

☐ lose sleep over this person

☐ are reduced to tears on more than one occasion

☐ spend a lot of time thinking about this relationship

☐ comply with the other person's unreasonable requests even when you are highly inconvenienced or sick

☐ take medications to cope with this relationship

☐ seek professional help

☐ sacrifice time in other relationships or activities

☐ miss work because this person needs you to do something for him or her

☐ change your schedule in order to accommodate him or her

☐ feel pressured to do unpleasant things you thought you would never do

☐ always seem to be defending yourself when you're around him or her

List some other things you have done in response to this person:

_____

_____

_____

_____

_____

Besides having a unique effect on how you behave and feel, a narcissist will have a strong impact on your thoughts. These thoughts can reveal much about your relationship.

Exercise: How Does Your Thinking Change in Response to the Narcissist?

Place a checkmark next to any of the following thoughts that that you have had in response to the narcissistic person:

☐ He or she is humiliating you on purpose.

☐ You are just not that important.

☐ You are stuck in this relationship.

☐ You are very stupid for staying in this relationship.

☐ You should be loyal and faithful and not leave this relationship.

☐ This person never plays by the rules.

☐ If you don't keep your guard up all the time, he or she will exploit you for sure.

☐ This relationship is the worst thing that could ever happen to you.

☐ You are so stupid for letting this person get to you.

☐ You just can't compete with him or her.

☐ You can never change the situation.

☐ If you let him or her, this person would entirely dominate you.

☐ The reason that this relationship doesn't go your way is because of your own defects.

☐ Somehow you did something to deserve this.

☐ As long as the other person is around, you will never get what you want.

☐ The situation will never end; it will always be the same.

☐ At times, this person wishes to demean you.

☐ This person will use you, no matter what you do.

☐ You can never please his or her.

☐ If only you could change somehow and become more like this person wants you to be, things would be much better.

☐ You are attracted to this relationship like a moth to a flame.

☐ Being around this person somehow makes you more important.

☐ You will never get through to this person; you can never get your point across.

☐ This person is so talented or gifted that you have to support him or her in these endeavors.

☐ This person couldn't care less about your feelings.

List some other thoughts you have had in response to this person:

_____

_____

_____

_____

_____

Look over your responses to these three exercises carefully. Did you check off many of the items? So what do you think? Remember, narcissists change the way you think, feel, and behave. Do you believe that your thoughts, feelings, and behaviors with this person are very different from those you have with other significant people in your life? Do you find that you are really not yourself when interacting with this person? If so, you are most likely dealing with a narcissist.

THE NARCISSIST TAKES ADVANTAGE OF YOU

In addition to making you feel, behave, and think in certain ways that are different from how you are with others, the narcissist will most likely have done things to you that others have not. Narcissists can be very exploitative, crossing over commonly accepted boundaries to take advantage of those around them.

Here's an example: A neighborhood group of men in their twenties used to get together sometimes to play poker, and they also played flag football with other neighborhood groups. The man who started the football team was a less-than-gifted athlete and card player and also a narcissist. He designated himself captain of the team and would always put himself in the skill positions, while benching those with real talent. During the group's card games, he would exaggerate his achievements during long discourses on the last game. When playing cards, he almost never had enough money to play and "borrowed" money from others, never paying them back. During one card game, a neighbor was talking about his new car, which he had just purchased that week. The narcissist began to insist that his neighbor lend him the car so he could drive to Florida—a thousand miles away—for a weeklong vacation because the narcissist's car was older and not as comfortable. When the neighbor refused, an argument ensued with the narcissist holding fast to the idea that there really was no reason for his neighbor not to lend the car. As tempers flared, others took the neighbor's side, and one person finally—and rightfully—accused the narcissist of never paying back the money he owed. The narcissist stormed out of the room. Afterward, the narcissist quit the card game and the football team, never to return again. In fact, he never spoke to any of the other men again, and when he eventually moved to a new neighborhood, he told his new neighbors that the people in the old neighborhood were just a bunch of whiners and cheaters.

The narcissist's voracious sense of entitlement makes it easy for him to exploit those around him; after all, he is such an exceptional person, he deserves what he takes. They should have given it to him in the first place.

Exercise: Is the Person in Your Life Exploitative?

Each of the following statements describes how a narcissist may be exploitative. Fill in the blanks using a scale of 1 to 5:

1	2	3	4	5
Strongly Disagree	Disagree	Neither Agree or Disagree	Agree	Strongly Agree

_____ 1. He or she takes or borrows money without paying it back.

_____ 2. This person takes credit for something that he or she did not do.

_____ 3. He or she requests special sexual favors.

_____ 4. He or she takes things without asking first.

_____ 5. This person destroys or ruins things of yours that he or she never offers to fix or replace.

_____ 6. He or she physically abuses you or others.

_____ 7. He or she makes sexual advances toward someone you had a romantic interest in.

_____ 8. This person spreads rumors about you or misrepresents you in some way so that he or she will look good.

_____ 9. This person insists that you participate in one of his or her self-serving agendas.

_____ 10. He or she insists that you do something unpleasant or highly inconvenient.

_____ 11. He or she insults, belittles, or injures those you are close to, usually without apology.

_____ 12. He or she breaks rules that apply to everyone else.

_____ 13. This person asks one of your acquaintances to do something unpleasant or inconvenient in spite of the fact that he or she barely knows that person.

_____ 14. This person lies to you for his or her own personal gain.

_____ 15. He or she makes you look foolish or stupid in the company of others (such as making you the butt of a joke or telling an embarrassing story about you).

Now add up the score. A score of over 55 suggests that the person in your life is exploitative.

Now list some specific instances in which this person has tried to exploit you or taken advantage of you. Examples might be "Even though we have broken up, he wants me to come over when he is sick to clean his wounds and get his medications." Or "My narcissist father is constantly hitting on my girlfriends, insisting they massage his shoulders because they are sore. He hugs them way too long and too close. He's twenty-five years older than them!"

Your examples:

_____

_____

_____

_____

_____

_____

_____

_____

_____

Time for some self-reflection. Does the fact that the person in your life exploits you and others because he or she feels entitled to do so make you see things a little differently? What has changed? How will having this knowledge enable you to act differently when this person takes advantage of you? Don't worry if you can't think of anything right now. This topic will be thoroughly covered in later chapters.

THE NARCISSIST ENGAGES IN SPLITTING BEHAVIORS

Psychologists use the term *splitting* to refer to the process of seeing the world in black-and-white terms with no gradations of gray. Splitting is a tendency to overvalue people, events, ideas, products, activities, and just about anything else you could name, only to quickly devalue these things after finding any type of flaw in them. People who do this see others in their lives as either wonderful or awful, helpful or useless, sexy or repulsive, winners or losers. There is no middle ground for them. If the narcissist in your life has this tendency, you are either a genius or a moron, someone she can either idolize or walk all over.

It is important to note here that the consistent use of splitting as a defense mechanism is usually the sign of a serious disorder. For example, it is frequently seen with borderline personality disorder, which is a disorder not unrelated to narcissism. While the discussion of this disorder is beyond the scope of this book, suffice it to say that people with borderline personality disorder are best known for being involved in astoundingly disturbed and tempestuous relationships, which are in large part fueled by the process of splitting. The concept of splitting is applicable to all types of narcissistic relationship problems, and understanding how it works with narcissism is critical to disarming a narcissist and disengaging from his toxic agendas.

One of the keys to understanding narcissism in the person you know is to recognize that the narcissist engages in splitting not only with others but also with himself. This will help you to get a handle on the other person's seemingly contradictory moods and behaviors, which may appear to change on a dime. For example, one narcissistic salesman felt that to be competent, he would need to sell a million dollars' worth of product in a three-month period. If he succeeded in this, he would be at the top of the world. He would date the most attractive women in town and compete in his favorite sport, which was racing motorboats. He would work out at the gym, honing his body to Olympian proportions while dressing only in the finest clothing. If he sold even a hundred dollars less than his million-dollar goal, however, he would go into a period of self-loathing, where he would just lie around all day, ignoring his hobbies and his social life and feeling he was an ugly, despicable failure. It was only during this time that he would seek out a therapist to help restore his self-esteem.

It may be some small consolation to know that what the narcissist does to others he also does to himself. But, you may wonder, where does splitting originate? Many psychologists believe that splitting is an early form of information processing. Very young children understand the world only in terms of black and white; fine variations and subtle gradations are far too complex for their young minds to grasp, and seeing them requires further brain development. It is important to recognize here that all of us have tendencies to split under certain conditions. For example, we tend to highly overvalue food when we are hungry; food that would usually disgust us may suddenly look awfully good. When we are in a rush to get to our jobs and the highways are bumper-to-bumper, everybody looks like an idiot, and it's really hard to find any use for other people whatsoever.

Splitting is one of the many psychological defense mechanisms people use when they feel threatened in some way. But narcissistic people can seem to be somewhat stuck in this information-processing mode.

With the narcissist, splitting can be extreme. Perhaps this is because narcissists are constantly living in a veiled but nonstop state of desperation, with all of their alarm systems locked to red-alert status, warning them that their self-esteem is in critical jeopardy.

Exercise: Is the Person in Your Life a Splitter?

Each of the following statements describes how a narcissist may engage in splitting behavior. Fill in the blanks using a scale of 1 to 5:

1	2	3	4	5
Strongly Disagree	Disagree	Neither Agree or Disagree	Agree	Strongly Agree

_____ 1. He or she seems to either love you or hate you; there is no middle ground.

_____ 2. He or she seems to have a long trail of people in the past that are now despised.

_____ 3. In the beginning of your relationship, this person said wonderful things to you. Now it's only biting criticisms.

_____ 4. This person seems to get angry with you quickly and for no apparent reason.

_____ 5. Your relationship seems to have really high highs and really low lows.

_____ 6. This person can turn his or her emotions on or off in a heartbeat.

_____ 7. There seems to be no middle ground with this person; everything is over the top.

_____ 8. If you cross this person, he or she will write you off almost immediately.

_____ 9. He or she is quickly attracted to new people, places, and things, only to become discouraged with them just as quickly.

_____ 10. This person says hateful things to you when he or she is unhappy with you.

_____ 11. He or she is on a high after accomplishing something but is absolutely miserable when not doing as well.

_____ 12. He or she seems to change moods quite frequently; you never know what you're going to get.

_____ 13. God forbid that you make this person look bad; he or she will absolutely loathe you.

_____ 14. When this person likes somebody, he or she tends to put that person way up on a pedestal.

_____ 15. He or she appears to be incredibly jealous or envious of other people's possessions or successes.

Now add up the score. A score of 53 or above suggests that you might be dealing with someone who is splitting.

Now list some examples of how the narcissistic person in your life has exhibited splitting behaviors. Examples might be "When he first dated me, he would write poetry about how beautiful I was, but now he is always critical of the way I look, telling me I look like a fat pig." Or "When I was first hired, the boss said she would put me in charge of the entire East Coast dealership, telling me I was the most incredibly gifted manager she had ever met. Now, she blames every failure in our department on me and tells me I am lucky just to have a job!"

Your examples:

_____

_____

_____

_____

_____

_____

_____

_____

_____

_____

Stop to reflect for a moment. Does this information make you look at the narcissist a little differently? Many people who are involved with narcissists feel a sense of relief when they realize that they are not responsible for the other person's view of them as a fallen angel. It's not your fault that the other person once saw you as wonderful but then became severely disappointed in you. How do you feel? Will having this knowledge help you react differently when the narcissist in your life engages in splitting?

THE NARCISSISTIC WOUND

Surprisingly, in spite of their bluster and arrogant personas, narcissists can be enormously sensitive to criticisms and personal failures. That grandiose and pompous exterior usually hides a frightened and ashamed little child who is petrified that his personal inadequacies will be exposed. This revelation can be shocking to almost anyone involved with a narcissist: "Are you kidding me? That self-infatuated, egotistical, and overconfident jerk of a boyfriend of mine who hits on anything with a skirt? Ashamed as a little child?" Yet it is all too true. If you think about it, it makes a lot of sense.

So, how did that ashamed little child grow up to be this self-centered, egotistical maniac? Karen Horney (1991) gives a very clear and simple explanation of this progression. As a young child, the narcissist has, like all of us, her own unique personality filled with her own matchless feelings, needs, and perceptions. This is what Horney calls the real self; it is the narcissist's true identity. Problems arise, however, when a key person in the child's life—almost always a parent—does not validate (or even like or approve of) all or part of the child's personality and therefore is rejecting. Disapproval may take the form of malicious criticisms, withdrawals of love, shaming, and all other types of cruel and insensitive rejection. The child's real self then becomes her despised self; she simply hates herself for being, at first, a failure in her parent's eyes and, then later, in her own. She now devalues and hates anything real or genuine within herself: she comes to define herself as weak, stupid, lacking in talent, cowardly, blameworthy, and, in general, disgraceful.

One way to look at the despised self is that it is a gaping, bleeding wound that the narcissist is continually trying to shield at all costs. It is an incredibly painful and shameful wound indeed, and to have it exposed through the revealing of her shortcomings would be a torturous and devastating humiliation that is only second to a slow and painful death. This narcissistic wound is exceedingly deep and its never-ending defense is the very thing that drives the narcissist, like a shark that must continue to swim just to breathe. A narcissistic high-school drama coach who was hypersensitive about his weight once reported this revealing dream: he was stripped naked by a crowd, beaten until he bled all over, tied to a pole, and paraded through the streets as thousands of people lined up to jeer and humiliate him. That is a portrait of the despised self.

The narcissist's solution to this intolerable state of affairs is to create yet another identity, one that Horney calls the idealized self and which is an attempt to mask and compensate for the despised self. In other words, the idealized self is the narcissist's glorious solution to his despised self: Where he was once weak, he is now a hero—no, a superhero—undefeatable in all that he does. Where she was once unattractive, she is now charming, seductive, and irresistible, the next supermodel replete with adoring fans and paparazzi. And where he was once without talent, he is now the world's foremost authority on, well, you name it. Talk about overcompensation. Now take all these things and inflate them to even larger proportions—that's the idealized self.

Yet in the deepest parts of their psyches, narcissists are keenly aware from their circumstances that the idealized self is a big lie: They find out that the waitress that they were trying to impress by leaving large tips was really giggling at their bloated pomposity behind their backs; the novel they believed to be the next best seller is still not finished; and they were unable to achieve an erection the last three times they attempted to consummate their latest seduction. They were turned down for the second time for a promotion, their last friend on earth won't return their calls, and they still can't seem to lose that excess thirty pounds. Each one of these humiliations is like a jolting body punch of reality—more salt poured into the existing wounds of childhood. They have been exposed! Now they hate themselves even more. But rather than acknowledge their shortcomings as just being human foibles, narcissists will compensate with an even grander and more superior version of themselves. But this tactic will also soon fail, as it is even more unobtainable than the one before. The idealized self-image is an impossibly unattainable fantasy, which can only lead the narcissist into a series of humiliating defeats. The process repeats itself over and over: trying to be a superman, only to fail and suffer humiliation, then hating themselves and compensating again by fashioning an even greater superman—a never-ending vicious cycle. A sad aside is that what is left out in this whole process is an acceptance of their true self. Narcissists don't know who they really are.

Perhaps even more surprising is that narcissists will bring on personal attacks. Their pomposity invites—no, begs for—criticism and assault on their character by others; people just ache to be the ones to give narcissists their comeuppance.

When dealing with the narcissist, it is useful to remember that beneath that veneer of cocky self-confidence lies a narcissistic wound. It doesn't take much to access this wound. Thus, your narcissist can be easily hurt and humiliated by slights, rejections, and even minor criticisms.

Exercise: Does the Person in Your Life Have a Narcissistic Wound?

Each of the following statements describes how a narcissist may be wounded. Fill in the blanks using a scale of 1 to 5:

1	2	3	4	5
Strongly Disagree	Disagree	Neither Agree or Disagree	Agree	Strongly Agree

_____ 1. He or she seems to be overly sensitive.

_____ 2. This person gets angry when you disagree with him or her.

_____ 3. He or she can never be wrong.

_____ 4. He or she gets angry or sulks even when you try to give constructive criticism.

_____ 5. He or she seems to need constant reassurance.

_____ 6. He or she always seems to be fishing for compliments.

_____ 7. This person will rant and rage if someone has disagreed with or criticized him or her.

_____ 8. Sometimes he or she looks like a wounded little child.

_____ 9. Criticism seems to stun him or her.

_____ 10. This person will cut another person out of his or her life the moment that person disagrees or finds fault with him or her.

_____ 11. He or she never forgets a slight.

_____ 12. He or she counterattacks swiftly.

_____ 13. This person is constantly saying how wonderful he or she is, as if needing this self-reinforcement.

_____ 14. This person becomes guarded or defensive when talking about his or her shortcomings.

_____ 15. You feel that you have to choose your words very carefully or you will offend him or her in some way.

Now add up the score. A score of 52 or above suggests that this person has a narcissistic wound.

Now list some examples of how the person in your life has exhibited a narcissistic wound:

_____

_____

_____

_____

_____

_____

_____

_____

_____

Take another moment for reflection. Knowing that this person suffers from a narcissistic wound can go a long way in your managing situations with him. First, you will not blame yourself when he overacts—it's not your fault that he goes into rages. You will understand why it is so difficult for him to admit that he is wrong, for doing so only reinforces the idea that he is defective. You will understand his need to denigrate others. You also will grow to recognize that you will get further with the narcissist by addressing the hurt beneath the anger. For example, suppose your narcissistic wife is in a tirade because you spent too much time speaking with an attractive salesclerk. Instead of saying something like "You always accuse me of doing things that I haven't done," you can say something like "I'm so sorry I hurt you. I really didn't mean for it to look like I was flirting. That wouldn't be fair to you." You will find that this type of statement will go a long way in helping you manage your relationship.

After reading this chapter, your perceptions and interpretations of events have probably changed. Interactions that have baffled you in the past should now be making more sense. What is the most significant thing that you will take away from this chapter? How will you react differently to the person in your life when she exhibits the traits discussed here?

Congratulations! At this point you should have a pretty good handle on whether or not the person about whom you are concerned is narcissistic. The fog should be beginning to clear. The next chapter will look at how the concepts introduced here can be applied to all kinds of personal and work relationships.

CHAPTER 3

Narcissism in Personal Relationships and in the Workplace

Narcissistic people can be found in all walks of life. You can find them in your neighborhood, your school, your business, and, yes, even your own family. You may find them on the front page of the newspaper or on your TV screen, but it's when the narcissist gets up close and personal that the sparks really begin to fly. Having a narcissistic spouse, boss, friend, or relative can be exhausting. And each type of relationship brings its own special challenges. This chapter will cover three different types of narcissistic relationships: romantic, when you are involved with a narcissist; parental, when you have at least one narcissistic parent; and workplace, when you have a narcissistic coworker or boss. We wish to note here that although it is important for you to focus on the type of relationship that is affecting you the most, you should read about the others as well. Most of the factual information, advice, and exercises offered here can be applied across a spectrum of relationship types.

NARCISSISTS IN ROMANTIC RELATIONSHIPS

We would like to start this section off by being utterly and painfully blunt, so here goes: No one is more at risk when dealing with a narcissist than someone who's involved in a long-term romantic relationship with a narcissist. Within an intimate relationship, the narcissist has a bounty of opportunities across scores of personal interactions to do harm to a sincere, committed, and oh so vulnerable lover. Even by the most basic of definitions, intimacy requires that you clear away a part of yourself to make room for another. Think about it. To be able to vibrate with the feelings of our loved ones is a personality prerequisite for anyone involved in a devoted relationship. The total consumption of the narcissist with his own needs makes him the odds-on favorite to continuously disregard the needs of his partner. Indeed, many narcissists actually enjoy withholding the very thing their partner needs the most; this is a type of one-upmanship designed to keep those around them humbled.

It is easy to be beguiled by a narcissist. He naturally projects an alluring guise of charisma, prestige, charm, and self-confidence. She reminds you of a movie star. He is the triumphant conqueror, a natural-born leader. She appears unflappable, handling all situations with unmitigated cool. There seems to be excitement wherever the narcissist goes, and you want to bask in the warmth of his radiance. When you are in her crosshairs, her expressions of quixotic passions can be infinitely infectious.

In the beginning, the narcissist will astound you by fulfilling all of your romantic fantasies in a whirlwind of romance. The lovemaking is intense and passionate; she will do everything she can to satisfy and impress you. He'll take you to must-see concerts and the trendiest restaurants, to the most expensive and notable nightspots and Broadway plays. ("*The Little Mermaid* was my favorite story as a little girl! How sweet.") He'll honor your birthday with an extravagant celebration and lavish gifts. Heck, he'll celebrate your mother's birthday with lavish gifts. ("Isn't he just wonderful? Now there's the man you should marry!") He will write you love letters infused with declarations of his eternal devotion to you, rivaling the poetry of the masters: you are his soul mate. He will create compilations of your favorite music. He will captivate you for evenings on end with his witty and clever jokes and his riveting stories of action-packed escapades, starring mostly, ahem…him.

The narcissist may have been attracted to you because she believed that you enhanced her image in some way, or she saw you as someone who was as wonderful as she was, her "heterosexual twin," so to speak (Akhtar 2009, 187). Perhaps he saw you as exceptionally beautiful, a partner who could fulfill his innermost passions, giving him the love he never really had. Maybe she believed that you were one of the few who could appreciate her inimitably superior gifts and visions of a perfect love. Or to him, you were a sex goddess, someone who would fulfill his wildest sexual fantasies. Upon first meeting you, he idealized you and put you up on the highest pedestal, a splendid prize to be seduced and won over and someone who would fill the emptiness inside, compensating for all of his shortcomings. His imagination exploded with vibrant fantasies, such as the two of you walking into a crowded room with you on his arm and everyone noticing what an incredible man this is who could win over this woman.

Even as early as the courtship phase, however, you may have noticed that your partner tended to dominate the conversation a little too often, brag a lot, and become very animated when talking about himself, and that he always had to get the better of someone. Start talking about yourself, and he started to look in the other direction, a process referred to as "glazing over" (Campbell 2005, 68).

For the narcissist, it is all about using you for his own needs while sucking you dry. The narcissist is a vampire on an endless journey to drain the energy out of others. He is always hunting for someone to meet his needs, to fill the emptiness inside, to affirm him as someone who is extraordinary and incomparable and to pump up his deflated self-esteem. The narcissist needs someone to applaud her accomplishments, to honor her cleverness; you are a special type of confidant and one of the few in the world who is capable of understanding and appreciating her uniqueness. She needs you to join her in appreciating all the finer things in life, to appreciate her expert tastes in music, art, fashion, style, and so on. Or he needs you to tell him that he's the best lover in the world and that no one could satisfy you the way that he does. Or perhaps the narcissist just needs a whipping boy, someone to blame and to take out his frustrations on—someone to take the fall for the emptiness he feels.

When the narcissist finds out that you cannot be his fantasy—no human being on earth could—he will go back on the hunt, which he really never gave up. Narcissists are notorious for secretly keeping all their options open; they are always looking for a better deal, a better relationship. Commitment is anathema. Better to leave all options open.

Exercise: How Did the Narcissist Use You to Gratify Certain Needs?

For the narcissistic romantic partner, it's always about fulfilling his or her own needs and little about meeting yours. Check off the needs a narcissistic romantic partner has sought to gratify through you.

☐ 1. Your partner knew he or she could control you.

☐ 2. Your partner believed your physical appearance would make him or her look even better.

☐ 3. Your partner needed an audience.

☐ 4. You were simply another one of his or her conquests.

☐ 5. You made your partner feel sexually desirable.

☐ 6. Your partner thought you would fulfill his or her sexual fantasies

☐ 7. Your partner needed someone to criticize and berate.

☐ 8. Your partner believed you could share in his or her superior tastes.

☐ 9. Your partner saw you as an exceptional provider.

☐ 10. Your partner saw you as a trophy husband or wife.

☐ 11. Your partner liked to show you off.

☐ 12. Your partner needed a "special friend" (narcissists have few—if any—true friends).

☐ 13. Your partner just used you for sex.

☐ 14. Your partner needed you to provide excitement in his or her life (or to join him or her in pursuing drama and excitement).

If your partner has tried to use you in other ways, please write them in the space provided:

_____

_____

_____

_____

_____

_____

_____

Exploitation is one of the key symptoms of narcissism; being used and taken advantage of is one of the hazards of being involved with a narcissist. If your partner is narcissistic, he will almost always take advantage of you in some way. If you rebuff these efforts, he will begin to see you as a less viable partner, a process psychologists call devaluation.

The Process of Devaluation

Soon after the courtship is over, narcissists typically begin to become disillusioned with their romantic partners. As the relationship progresses and the narcissist learns more factual information about you, he will discover that you are really only human and not the goddess he initially saw you as. This can be devastating for the narcissist; you, in all your humanness, will never be able to be her equal, will never be able to relate to and appreciate his extraordinary type of genius. The narcissist begins, then, to find fault with you, at first asking you to "lose a few pounds," "cut your hair," "dress more like your girlfriend," "stop interrupting me when I speak," or all of the above. But as time goes on, the attacks become more long-winded and vitriolic: you are "nothing but a clingy little child," "fat, ugly and stupid," "an embarrassment and are holding me back from my destiny of fame and fortune," or "the worst mistake I ever made in my life." Or "You disgust me. You'll hear from my attorneys." Yup, devaluation can be a little rough on your self-esteem.

At this point, the narcissist has flipped the switch and turned off his feelings for you. He may have already found another person to pursue. Narcissists love the act of seduction, and many will not commit to a relationship, for they are in love with falling in love—it's a daily fix—but are incapable of doing the real work of maintaining a true intimate bond.

Exercise: How Did the Narcissist Devalue You?

Check off the problems below that you have had with a narcissistic romantic partner after the courtship was over.

☐ 1. Your partner became critical of your physical appearance.

☐ 2. Your partner saw your friends as inferior or low class.

☐ 3. Your partner began to complain about your family members.

☐ 4. Your partner judged your tastes and preferences as second-rate.

☐ 5. Your partner perceived the differences between the two of you as a problem.

☐ 6. Your partner saw you as an intellectual inferior.

☐ 7. Your partner wanted you to do more for the relationship than he or she did.

☐ 8. Your partner wanted you to do all of the changing.

☐ 9. Your partner began to find fault with your lovemaking.

☐ 10. Your partner began to make decisions for you.

☐ 11. Your partner told you what type of opinions to have.

☐ 12. Your partner expected you to show deference.

☐ 13. Your partner was critical of the way you dressed.

☐ 14. Your partner did not like the way you behaved in public.

☐ 15. Your partner made unilateral decisions that affected both of you in big ways, such as where to live or what type of car you should buy.

☐ 16. Your partner began comparing you to former lovers.

☐ 17. Your partner began looking at other attractive women or men.

☐ 18. Your partner seemed to put other people down a lot as well.

☐ 19. Your partner wouldn't take responsibility for things he or she said, claiming something was a joke or denying it entirely.

☐ 20. Your partner developed other relationships that you did not trust as innocent, for example, "an old friend" contacted on the Internet.

☐ 21. Your partner began to blame others too.

☐ 22. You began to feel intimidated by your partner.

☐ 23. Your partner began to accuse you of things you didn't do.

☐ 24. Your partner tried to change you into something you weren't.

☐ 25. You felt you could not live up to your partner's expectations.

The stings of devaluation can be hurtful, but remember that they are lies used by the narcissist to maintain his own self-esteem. And remember, it is also a lie when the narcissist sees you as perfect. It is seductive and intoxicating indeed when the narcissist puts you up on a pedestal by overvaluing you. But, like any drug, the hangover of devaluation soon follows. The obvious lesson here might be not to drink in the overvaluation in the first place.

Female Narcissists in Romantic Relationships

While most narcissists are men, approximately 30 percent are women. And while the underlying motivations and dynamics of female narcissists are the same as for men, there are some characteristics specific to female narcissism worth discussing here.

More often than not, a female narcissist will be physically appealing and even strikingly beautiful. Throughout her childhood, people most likely told her how lovely she looked, and right from the start, she felt she was special and therefore deserving of special treatment. She might have had a "stage mother," who promoted the idea that she was someone out of the ordinary and destined for celebrity and fame. During her school years, she was typically the queen bee, the beauty with whom all the other girls longed to be friends. But she was also that mean girl who enlisted sympathizers to torment and denigrate her rivals and others whom she deemed to be beneath her; a female bully who used words rather than fists to beat up those she found irritating. In high school, she only dated the most handsome and admired boys—the football stars and class presidents—only to become easily bored or disappointed with them: "How dare he not fall all over me when we were with his new friends?" She would then move on quickly toward her next conquest, fending off her rivals in new fits of envy and rage, taking every opportunity to demean them and destroy their reputations.

In college, she sought out only the most popular students and prestigious activities, often jumping from one to the next in her desperate search for enough attention, compliments, pledges of devotion, adulation, and self-worship. She would swear to her latest beau that the army of male suitors around her was made up of just friends, while insulting him for his petty jealousies and small-mindedness.

With an eye toward marriage, she looks for a rising star—perhaps a narcissist in his own right—who will not only enthrone her in the fervor of his devotion but who will lay at her feet the riches of the world. Narcissistic wives fantasize about impressing friends with the beauty of their homes and possessions: "This gown? Oh, so nice of you to notice. It's a Michael Kors original. God bless that man. I so love his use of textures. We met him in Bangkok—is that correct, Richard, or was it Paris? Paris has gotten soooo boring."

As a mother, she has far-fetched expectations of her children. Most likely recognizing that she hasn't yet achieved stardom in her own right, she sees her possibilities through her offspring, who soon find that it is next to impossible to please her. Ironically, while narcissistic mothers see their children as an extension of themselves, they often see their daughters as rivals and can become jealous over the attention their father gives them. Similar to their male counterparts, narcissistic women can be notoriously moody. They can get very angry and go into rages if they feel they are losing control. They will become verbally and even physically abusive to their partner, and they know just how to cut the other person to the quick.

Finally, as a female narcissist begins to age and lose her youthful beauty, she will become even more frantic in her self-absorption, searching for ways to restore her youth: a different gym, more yoga and

Pilates, perhaps a new personal trainer, cosmetic surgery, and maybe a younger lover. She redoubles her efforts to control those around her, dictating her children's wedding plans, for example, or joining a new social club so she can be the president. Old admirers desert her, exacerbating her loneliness. She can become a chronic complainer, destroying her few remaining relationships.

NARCISSISTS AS PARENTS

Narcissistic parenting can be exceptionally devastating, given the vulnerability and helplessness of small children and the incredible amount of control parents have over them. Children need to feel free to develop their own identities and to flourish in their own special way, a task next to impossible when in the shadows of a self-absorbed parent. The children of narcissistic parents must endure an entire spectrum of narcissistic symptomatology at a time when their neural pathways are most impressionable, and as a result, the impact of their parent's behavior will forever affect their behavioral, emotional, and thought patterns. While we believe that anyone involved with a narcissist can benefit from professional help, adult children of narcissistic parents should most seriously consider it, particularly for help with intimate relationships, where toxic narcissistic parenting can have the greatest impact.

The child of a narcissistic parent is often an extension of his parent's wild fantasies of success; the parent expects her child to be exceptionally talented and gifted and to always achieve excellence. As no child can ever really live up to these fantastic expectations, the children of narcissists tend to suffer from chronic feelings of low self-esteem and never being quite good enough. The narcissistic parent will often ridicule and demean the child for his failures, putting him on a roller-coaster ride of idealization and devaluation—the process of splitting. The narcissistic parent will often try to keep the child in a one-down position by reminding the child of her shortcomings: "No man is going to want you if you don't start losing weight. When I was your age, I already had seven boyfriends." A disappointed narcissistic parent will withhold affection and other nurturance, constantly offer criticisms and put-downs, and, especially when the child is older, withhold material resources: this parent will cut a child off in a heartbeat once the child lets her down. When children confront their parents with these behaviors, they're most likely to hear that they are misperceiving the facts or being overly sensitive. Rarely do the children of narcissists receive adequate credit for the things they have achieved, while, ironically, their parents will often brag about how wonderful these children are to their friends and associates.

In addition to personal attacks, the children of narcissists must suffer the fallout from the inevitable clashes between narcissistic parents and other family members, conflicts that often include emotional and physical abuse.

NARCISSISTS IN THE WORKPLACE

If you are working with a narcissistic coworker or boss, the level of the severity of the problem will vary depending on how much contact you must have with that person and how much power and authority he has over you. The rest of this chapter will discuss some difficult traits that you may find in a narcissist at work.

The Narcissist Has Star Quality

The narcissistic in the workplace initially impresses others as very charismatic, authoritative, confident, and entertaining. People are naturally drawn toward him and the excitement he creates. Coworkers will often talk about how wonderful or talented he is, even to the point of envy. If he has an audience, he will launch into long-winded and theatrical monologues so laced with (faked) noble passion that the listener will think she is listening to Patrick Henry's "Give me liberty or give me death" speech. Often, this shooting star quickly fades, not having the skills or strength of character necessary to really succeed. Always remember, narcissists live to be admired. The narcissist, seeing himself as such a wonderful person to work with, might even acknowledge your admiration and throw you a bone every once in a while. Don't mistake this for real friendship.

Exercise: Has a Narcissist in Your Workplace Shown Star Quality?

List some of the ways a narcissist in your workplace has demonstrated star quality. Were you attracted to the narcissist because of his or her charisma?

_____

_____

_____

_____

_____

_____

The Narcissist Is Domineering

A narcissistic coworker will most likely be the one taking over meetings and advancing her own agendas. Get in her way and she'll try to run over you. She will interrupt you, dismiss you, ignore you, and demean you—anything to avoid having to listen to your concerns. She is a master at one-upmanship and will do almost anything to get a leg up on the competition, including spreading lies and rumors, forming malevolent alliances (which can often include befriending an enemy's enemies), violating rules that get in her way, taking credit for things she did not do, and grabbing equipment and resources—such as the best office space—to enhance her status. If you decide to take this narcissist on, you will have your hands full. Be prepared for an "I don't get mad, I get even" attitude. The effects of these behaviors are magnified when this person is your boss who, by definition, has more control over your life.

Exercise: Has a Narcissist in Your Workplace Been Domineering?

List some of the ways the narcissist in your workplace has been domineering. How do you feel about that now?

_____

_____

_____

_____

_____

_____

The Narcissist Lacks Empathy

Usually professing just the opposite ("I feel your pain"), a narcissistic coworker or boss will be insensitive to your needs. His starting assumption is that his needs are more important than yours. He will have no desire to fill in for you when you need him to or give you needed sick time or a vacation-time preference. He will not appreciate the fact that you are overworked and underpaid. Your agenda will always be second to his. When the child of a faculty member was involved in a serious accident and the faculty member had to cancel her classes in order to rush to the hospital, her narcissistic department head scolded her, telling her she needed to make a choice between her children and the university. Want to be respected and treated fairly? Forget about it!

Exercise: Has a Narcissist in Your Workplace Lacked Empathy?

List some of the ways the narcissist in your workplace has shown a lack of empathy. How do you feel about that now?

_____

_____

_____

_____

_____

_____

The Narcissist Seeks High-Status People, Activities, or Positions

The narcissist loves to bask in the spotlight of admiration. Some narcissists may indeed be natural leaders if their narcissism is not too bad. But many narcissists are drawn to high-status positions solely because of the glory it brings them. Narcissists are drawn to leadership roles, such as labor leader, department or committee head, or coach of a recreational sports team. When one narcissistic woman was asked why she applied for the job of shop steward, she replied, "So I can be the queen and tell people what to do." You will see the narcissist sucking up to the real leaders of the organization; he will make no secret about how he took the big boss out on a golf outing and, with a wink, "let him win." Oh, by the way, did he mention that he's vacationing with one of the board members?

Exercise: Has a Narcissist in Your Workplace Sought High Status?

List some of the ways the narcissist in your workplace has been drawn to people, things, or activities that connoted high status or prestige. How did you or your coworkers respond?

_____

_____

_____

_____

_____

The Narcissist Is a Teacher, Not a Mentor

Self-centered people like to see themselves as being giving and magnanimous. The narcissist in your workplace may share information with you, especially if it makes her feel superior to you in some way. She will often instruct you on how to do things like get around the folks in accounting or work the company's new netbooks or tell you where the best eateries are. But once she has impressed you, her job is over. If you go back for further help or explanation, she will most likely think that you are a complete idiot for not having gotten it the first time around.

Exercise: What Has a Narcissist in Your Workplace Tried to Teach You?

List what the narcissist in your workplace has tried to teach you. Did you feel he or she was really trying to help you or was just trying to impress you? If you knew then what you now know, how might have you behaved?

_____

_____

_____

_____

_____

_____

_____

The Narcissist Demands Special Treatment

The narcissist has an insatiable appetite for special treatment and believes he is entitled to it. He will demand the best office, the first available and most desirable vacation times, and the first of the brand-new laptops being issued. He should be the first to receive any extra monies, supplies, or perks. He will demand everything that he believes he deserves while stubbornly refusing to acknowledge the rights and feelings of others. And he's not afraid to cross legal or ethical boundaries because, after all, "Aren't you just one of those bean counters in accounting?"

Exercise: Has a Narcissist in Your Workplace Demanded Special Treatment?

List some of the ways the narcissist in your workplace has asked for or received special treatment. How did you or your coworkers react to this?

_____

_____

_____

_____

_____

_____

_____

The Narcissist Has Love-Hate Relationships

If a narcissistic coworker or boss sees you as a person who might be beneficial to her in some way, she will idealize you and see you as absolutely wonderful and perfect. (Careful now, you just might believe this. Narcissists have a wonderful way of tapping into your own sense of self-importance.) She will covet your friendship. But when you do not live up to that image of perfection that she has of you, you will become a complete zero in her mind. This is an example of splitting. Was it because you "betrayed" her by disagreeing with her at a union meeting? You viper, you! Was it because you were talking to one of her enemies? Traitor! Why has she been avoiding you lately? You might never know, for it could have been anything—like just being a human being.

Exercise: Have the Feelings of a Workplace Narcissist Changed Dramatically Toward You?

List some instances in which the narcissist's feelings toward you have vacillated between love and hate:

_____

_____

_____

_____

_____

_____

_____

The Narcissist Exploits Others

The narcissist believes he has an inalienable right to whatsoever he desires, and it is this colossal sense of entitlement—after all, he is so wonderful, gifted, and special—that allows him to bend or break the rules that are commonly shared in a corporate setting. When you couple this sense of entitlement with the narcissist's ability to captivate and charm, you have a perfect storm wherein the narcissist will ruthlessly take advantage of others. Rules do not seem to apply to him; rather, they are for the common folk. He does not respect the personal rights of others but sees them as obstacles. Narcissists have been known to cheat on their time sheets, pad their expenses, take credit for the work of others, sexually exploit coworkers, steal, wantonly disregard the duties and obligations that are part of their job description, and, in general, have the unalterable conviction that they deserve much more than they have been getting.

When a narcissistic manager took advantage of his incredibly young and impressionable secretary by having a series of sexual escapades with her, his own administrator asked him how he could be so callous. His reply was "Believe me, she got the better of the deal." That kind of sums it all up, doesn't it?

Exercise: Have You Been Exploited by a Narcissist in Your Workplace?

List how you have been exploited by a narcissistic coworker or boss. What were your feelings, thoughts, and behaviors during those times?

_____

_____

_____

_____

_____

_____

The Narcissist Trolls for Validation

The narcissistic coworker typically walks around with a huge hole inside that she is always trying to fill: every day she searches in desperation for a fix of supplies to boost her self-esteem. For example, being relatively devoid of anything very original of her own to contribute, she is always looking to steal ideas from her colleagues. Perhaps it is someone else's idea to improve management-employee relationships or a new idea for the design of an employee manual. It could be insider information, by which she can scoop the other gossips in the organization, or a well-turned phrase she can pass off as her own. It could be a new advertising campaign or ways to improve distribution—anything to make her look special.

The narcissist will need emotional validation as well. He needs to be told he is sexy, brilliant, superior to others, and an irreplaceable employee. You'll hear him say, "Hey, how much did you love how I put Frank in his place today?" Or "Bet this place never saw numbers like mine before, huh?" Or "What's a guy to do when he's so irresistible to women?" He's always on the prowl.

Exercise: What Validation Does the Narcissist in Your Workplace Seek?

List some instances in which a narcissistic coworker or boss has sought validation from you. What was your reaction?

_____

_____

_____

_____

_____

_____

The preceding exercises were designed to show you how narcissistic tendencies can make someone a handful to deal with at work. Were you able to identify certain of these tendencies in your narcissistic coworker or boss? Now that you recognize these qualities, do you feel differently toward this person or toward yourself?

At this point, we hope that you have been able to identify the narcissistic tendencies that are in your relationship, whether the narcissist you know is someone close to you or someone you work with. The next chapter looks specifically at how the narcissist in your life affects you; it also gives specific strategies for managing these incredibly self-centered people.

CHAPTER 4

How the Narcissist Affects You

The goal of this chapter is to help you examine how you react to the narcissist in your life. You need to understand your own reactions before you can figure out how to respond differently. First, here are a couple of stories about people who are dealing with a narcissist in their lives. As you read their stories, try to imagine how these people might be feeling. What emotions arise? Do these responses remind you of your own?

◆ Cindy's Story

Cindy has been working for Veronica for the past two years at a retail clothing manufacturer. At first, Cindy was impressed by Veronica's ability to handle herself in a variety of situations with both clients and employees, but she soon began to see her in a different light. This first occurred when Cindy came up with an idea for how to cut down on employee absenteeism, suggesting that she and her coworkers submit requests for their preferred days off prior to the work schedule coming out. Apparently, this plan was highly successful for both the employees and the company. A few months afterward, however, Cindy learned from one of the district managers that Veronica had not only taken credit for Cindy's suggestion but also received a pretty substantial bonus. Cindy was outraged. She made hints to Veronica, hoping that Veronica would admit to having stolen Cindy's idea, but Veronica never did. Cindy became totally exasperated and one day confronted Veronica about what she had heard. Veronica replied that she never recalled having such a conversation with Cindy about the work schedule and that it was her own idea. Again, Cindy was outraged. As if to add insult to injury, the following week Cindy found out from the district manager that she was being demoted and transferred to another store that was a forty-mile commute from her home.

◆ Jean's Story

Jean and her sister Marilyn were quite close growing up, probably because they were only two years apart. When Marilyn, the younger of the two, went off to college, Jean resented that Marilyn was given the opportunity to go away to school whereas she'd had to work and go to the local community college. Marilyn always acted very haughty and arrogant and felt she was better than Jean and her mother, yet Marilyn had always been her mother's favorite. When Jean and Marilyn's father had died when they were still in high school, their mother had come to rely on Jean even more for help with household chores as well as paying the bills and keeping the finances in order. Once Marilyn had graduated from college, she got a high-paying job in a Manhattan bank and would only visit her mother and Jean on occasion. When her mother was diagnosed with cancer, it was Jean who took her to the oncologist and to her radiation treatments and made sure she received the best care possible. Marilyn was so busy with her job that she only came to visit her mother once after she was diagnosed. Was it any surprise that Marilyn was left just about everything in her mother's will, including the house, the car, and her mother's jewelry, while Jean was given a few pieces of furniture? Naturally, Marilyn felt that she was entitled to everything and promptly sold the house and other valuables to purchase a condo in Aspen.

These two situations illustrate how difficult it can be to keep your emotional bearings when dealing with a narcissist. We are personally aware of situations where people have quit their jobs, cut off all contact with family members, or even bought voodoo dolls as a means of breaking off contact with a narcissist who has made their lives miserable. And what often makes matters worse is that the narcissist will either have no idea of how offensive his behavior has been or will feel entitled to act the way he does because he thinks he is special.

HOW PEOPLE RESPOND EMOTIONALLY TO NARCISSISTS

Although there are many variations, there are three main ways that most people tend to respond emotionally to narcissists. Most reactions can be grouped into the following categories:

Angry/Resentful	Denigrated/Intimidated	Apathetic/Detached
enraged	dejected	defeated
fuming	lacking self-esteem	lethargic
seething	guilty	tired
furious	degraded	indifferent
wrathful	humiliated	distant
ranting	worthless	removed

Here are some stories illustrating these responses in action:

◆ Marci's Story

Marci and David have been married for three years. Marci is a third-grade teacher and really loves her work and the children she teaches. David is an up-and-coming assistant district attorney. David constantly puts Marci down, picking on her about the way she dresses and about the high school and college friends she keeps in touch with. David never misses a chance to remind Marci that he makes more money than she does and that his job is more important than hers. Marci resents David's put-downs, but she has learned not to pay much attention to him when he is being critical. What has really infuriated Marci, however, is David's flirtatiousness with his female colleagues. One of her friends told her that she'd seen David out to dinner with one of these women when he was supposedly "working late." One evening, Marci decided to follow David when he was leaving the office and found him with one of these "colleagues," kissing in front of a neighborhood restaurant. Marci took a golf club from the trunk of her car and smashed out the windshield of David's new car.

◆ Jim's Story

Jim has worked for Sandra for the past four years. Sandra is the rising star of their corporation because of her sales numbers, which broke all corporate records. No one was surprised when she was promoted to vice-president of the sales department...no one except for Jim. A friend of his, who had worked for Sandra at her former employer, told Jim that Sandra had stolen away several clients and had racked up high sales numbers by cashing in on the clients she stole. Since being promoted, Sandra has been totally out of control. She treats Jim as if he were a piece of dirt, constantly criticizing him for every little thing he does. She accused him of padding his expense accounts and not keeping up with sales calls. Jim felt disparaged and maligned. At one point, when Jim went to speak with Sandra's boss, he was told that everyone thinks she is doing a wonderful job "whipping the sales force into shape" and that he should "either get on board or look for work elsewhere." Jim felt even more humiliated and dejected and regretted having spoken out.

◆ Christine's Story

Christine has been dating Jon for a couple of years. She remembers how impressed she was with him in the beginning of their relationship and how he would buy her expensive gifts and take her to fancy restaurants. After the first few months of their relationship, though, Christine noticed that Jon would become very short-tempered with her over little things. If she asked him if something were bothering him, Jon would just yell at her more. These temper outbursts continued to escalate to the point were Jon would threaten to hurt Christine. In response, Christine found herself watching everything she did or said but eventually felt there was "no pleasing Jon," for no matter how attentive or affectionate she was, there was no way to keep him from going into these fits of rage.

◆ Suzanne's Story

Suzanne is twenty-eight years old, single, and quite successful in her career, yet whenever she gets around her mother, she feels like she is seven years old again. Suzanne remembers from her childhood that her mother was incredibly self-centered, both in how she treated her father and in how she treated her younger sister and herself. Suzanne can recall thinking that "everything always revolves around Mom." Suzanne dreaded the Christmas holidays, when her mother would come down with her traditional holiday migraines so that she could avoid doing anything around the house to prepare for Christmas. Suzanne's father would do all the cooking, cleaning, and wrapping of presents. The same was true when they would go on summer vacation. Suzanne's mother was always preoccupied with her girlfriends at the club. Later, as an adult, Suzanne learned that her mother was having an affair, which really didn't surprise her. After her father died, Suzanne found herself being her mother's confidante and caretaker, a role she was reluctant to take on. At times she becomes infuriated at her mother, but she always feels guilty afterward for what she has said and returns to her caretaker role. The few times that Suzanne has become involved in serious dating relationships, her mother has found ways to sabotage them, by feigning illnesses when Suzanne has made plans to go out or wanted to go away for a romantic weekend. Suzanne has resigned herself to the fact that she will never have a life of her own as long as her mother is still alive.

In these stories, you can see how Marci, Jim, Christine, and Suzanne try to manage the narcissists in their lives. Marci is brought to the point of anger, frustration, and eventually rage by David's egocentric, philandering behavior, while Jim exemplifies those who are made to feel dejected and humiliated. Christine demonstrates what psychologists refer to as "learned helplessness" (Walker 2000), as she has come to the point of apathy about her relationship with Jon, knowing that there's nothing she can do or say to make it better.

It is also possible for you to respond differently depending on your nature, how you're feeling at the time, or what behavior you're responding to. For example, the type of philandering that Marci was enraged by might instead provoke a sense of apathy or detachment in someone else. Similarly, the type of put-downs to which Jim was subjected might provoke frustration or anger in someone else. Suzanne demonstrates how a person may go from one feeling to the next, from anger and frustration to guilt and even apathy, as she attempts to deal with an overbearing, narcissistic parent. What is common in all four scenarios is that narcissists have a unique talent for getting a rise out of those who come into contact with them.

Living with or being involved in a relationship with a narcissist over time can change how you think and react in different types of situations. This next exercise can help you see the extent to which this is happening in your life.

Exercise: How Do You Change in Response to the Narcissist in Your Life?

For each of the following statements, check off whether the situation described rarely, sometimes, often, or always happens to you.

1. You find yourself taking a backseat to the narcissist's wishes or desires, thereby forgoing your own.

   ☐   rarely happens

☐   sometimes happens

☐   often happens

☐   always happens

2.   When something goes wrong, the narcissist blames you for whatever the problem may be, and as a result, you are apprehensive and on guard about making mistakes.

☐   rarely happens

☐   sometimes happens

☐   often happens

☐   always happens

3.   You find yourself hiding your own feelings or thoughts because the narcissist usually discounts your opinions or how you feel.

☐   rarely happens

☐   sometimes happens

☐   often happens

☐   always happens

4.   You find that the narcissist uses your creativity, energy, or ideas for his or her own gain or will have you do things that he or she dislikes doing. As a result, you find yourself being emotionally withholding or distancing in the relationship.

☐   rarely happens

☐   sometimes happens

☐   often happens

☐   always happens

5.   You find yourself needing to bolster the narcissist's ego or offer reassurance. You will express admiration even when you don't want to. This makes you feel resentful.

☐   rarely happens

☐   sometimes happens

☐   often happens

☐   always happens

6.   You avoid asking things of the narcissist because you're afraid that you'll be told you're being selfish or demanding.

☐   rarely happens

☐ sometimes happens

☐ often happens

☐ always happens

7. You forgo making plans to do things for yourself because you feel you're at the narcissist's beck and call.

☐ rarely happens

☐ sometimes happens

☐ often happens

☐ always happens

8. You find yourself needing to defend the narcissist to others when they criticize him or her.

☐ rarely happens

☐ sometimes happens

☐ often happens

☐ always happens

9. You find yourself avoiding social engagements with the narcissist because you're afraid you may be embarrassed by what the narcissist may say or do.

☐ rarely happens

☐ sometimes happens

☐ often happens

☐ always happens

10. You avoid social events with the narcissist because of how the narcissist treats you when you're around other people, and you don't want to feel humiliated.

☐ rarely happens

☐ sometimes happens

☐ often happens

☐ always happens

Now take at look at your responses to the questions. If you've responded "often happens" or "always happens" to more than six of these questions, then you probably are being stressed by your relationship with a narcissist. It's likely you find yourself questioning whether the relationship will ever be an equal partnership or whether your needs will ever be met.

The next exercise will help you start a journal of your responses and reactions to various situations that may arise daily with the narcissist in your life.

Exercise: Keeping Track of Your Responses

Start by looking at the past week. Think of situations in which the narcissist in your life may have done things that set you off. Indicate what the situation was and then whether your emotional response was one of the following: angry/resentful, denigrated/intimidated, or apathetic/detached. If you didn't have any contact with that person on a particular day, simply state "no contact."

	Situation	Your Reaction
Sunday	_____	_____
	_____	_____
Monday	_____	_____
	_____	_____
Tuesday	_____	_____
	_____	_____
Wednesday	_____	_____
	_____	_____
Thursday	_____	_____
	_____	_____
Friday	_____	_____
	_____	_____
Saturday	_____	_____
	_____	_____

Now, over the coming week, keep another daily journal of situations in which the narcissist sets you off. Again document what happened with the narcissist and how you responded.

	Situation	Your Reaction
Sunday	_____	_____
	_____	_____
Monday	_____	_____
	_____	_____
Tuesday	_____	_____
	_____	_____
Wednesday	_____	_____
	_____	_____
Thursday	_____	_____
	_____	_____
Friday	_____	_____
	_____	_____
Saturday	_____	_____
	_____	_____

Now look at your lists for both weeks. Is there anything you notice about the types of situations you find yourself reacting to? Is there anything you notice about how you usually find yourself reacting? For example, do you find yourself usually feeling angry and resentful, or denigrated and intimidated, or apathetic and detached? List what you've noticed about your reactions:

_____

_____

_____

_____

If you could change anything about the way you react or respond to the narcissist, what would it be? Often therapists ask their clients to try something different or to try a little experiment in order to see if it changes the pattern of their interactions with the narcissist. Remember: Don't expect the narcissist to change.

Exercise: Reconsidering Your Response

Take any of the situations that you responded to and consider how you might have responded differently to that situation. Remember, in some instances changing how you respond may mean not responding at all. Linda Martinez-Lewi (2008) talks about the art of practicing restraint, which means that at times you may decide not to respond to narcissistic behavior, such as tirades or put-downs. Describe below how you may want to respond differently to the narcissist:

_____

_____

_____

_____

MOVING BEYOND CODEPENDENCE

You're probably familiar with the concept of codependency. It was originally applied to those who live and cope with someone who has an active addiction (for example, to alcohol, drugs, gambling, sex, or shopping). Simply put, the addict focuses his life around his drug of choice or addictive behavior while the codependent focuses his life around the addicted person. Most experts agree that codependency is a learned behavior that originates from having grown up in a dysfunctional family in which family life focuses on the person with the addiction (Beattie 1987, 1989). Although many professionals consider codependency to be a disease, in much the same way as addiction can be viewed as a disease, other professionals consider codependency to be an attempt to cope with a situation that has become maladaptive, dysfunctional, or intolerable. Similarly, living with a narcissist can create maladaptive, dysfunctional, and intolerable situations—and codependent behaviors.

What Does It Mean to Be Codependent?

Codependent reactions to a narcissistic spouse, partner, family member, or even boss or coworker are quite common. Very similar to living with or working with an addict or alcoholic, living or working with a narcissist often leaves people caught in the web of caring for a person whose life may be spinning out of control (while to the outside world the narcissist may appear to really have it all together).

So what does it mean to be codependent? Codependents will typically do the following:

◆ put others' needs before their own

◆ have trouble defining their feelings, wants, and needs

- feel guilty if not taking care of someone else

- find it difficult to accept compliments or gifts

- be in relationships in which they are treated abusively

- do anything to keep the relationship going

- look to others for reassurance even if they know they are right

- have difficulty completing projects because time is usurped by others

- think they are not worthwhile or lovable

- do more than their fair share in relationships

- try to please others at their own expense

- be attracted to needy people

- have difficulty making decisions without a lot of reassurance

- feel tired or exhausted most of the time because of taking care of others

The following exercise will help you determine if codependency is an issue in your relationship.

Exercise: Could You Be Codependent?

Simply respond to each statement by checking off "mostly true" or "mostly false" to describe your relationship with the narcissist in your life, or with other people.

mostly true   mostly false

_____   _____   1. Your spouse or partner would fall apart without you.

_____   _____   2. You do most of the work in your relationship.

_____   _____   3. You have trouble saying no to your partner or coworker.

_____   _____   4. You feel compelled to help the other person.

_____   _____   5. You try to anticipate your partner's or coworker's needs.

_____   _____   6. You feel responsible for the other person.

_____   _____   7. You try to please the other person at your own expense.

_____   _____   8. You find it easier to express anger over injustices done to the other person than to yourself.

_____ _____ 9. You check in with the other person more often than you check in with yourself.

_____ _____ 10. You often feel unappreciated but don't express it.

_____ _____ 11. You often feel guilty spending money on yourself.

_____ _____ 12. You often find yourself fearing rejection.

_____ _____ 13. You find it easier to do things for the other person than for yourself.

_____ _____ 14. You'll often stop something you're doing or working on to help the other person.

_____ _____ 15. You often find yourself being attracted to people who have a lot of problems.

If you answered "mostly true" to five or more of these statements, then chances are you may be codependent. Again, we cannot stress too strongly the idea that codependent reactions are common when dealing with people who manifest a great deal of unmanageability or dysfunction in their lives.

Have you taken on a codependent coping style to deal with living or working with someone with narcissistic traits? List any examples you can think of:

_____

_____

_____

_____

_____

_____

_____

PUTTING THINGS INTO PERSPECTIVE

Before moving on, there are a couple of things you need to take into account. First, narcissists don't wear signs announcing to the world that they are narcissistic. So it's not unusual to get taken in by a narcissist if you meet her socially or on the job. It's easy to be flattered by the attention the narcissist shows you. In other words, don't be hard on yourself for being in the clutches of a narcissist. Typically narcissists are quite skilled at reading people and creating a good first impression. This is one of the reasons why in work settings they rise to positions of power so quickly. This is also why in intimate relationships the interaction usually starts off very well. You may feel great about the attention or expressions of affection you're receiving, but most often these interactions turn sour within a sometimes-brief period. So again, don't blame yourself for getting sucked into a relationship with a narcissist. You're in good company.

One of the common elements to most relationships with narcissists is that they often start off being very exciting and satisfying, but over time, as the narcissist becomes more demanding, the balance of the relationship shifts. Sometimes this shift may be dramatic; at other times it may be subtle.

Exercise: How Has Your Relationship Changed?

Answer the following questions to see how your relationship with the narcissist has changed over time.

What was your relationship like in the beginning, when you first met?

_____

_____

_____

What was your relationship like at six months?

_____

_____

_____

What was your relationship like at one year?

_____

_____

_____

How has your relationship changed since then?

_____

_____

_____

At what point did you feel your relationship had changed dramatically?

_____

_____

_____

By now you should have a good understanding of narcissism and narcissistic personality traits. You've learned about the different subtypes of narcissists and about some of the contemporary theories for what causes narcissism. You have identified the narcissistic traits in your partner, friend, family member, or coworker and also examined how you may have responded to this narcissistic behavior. In part 2, you will learn some strategies for change.

PART 2

Practical Strategies

CHAPTER 5

Understanding What You Can and Cannot Change

The rest of this book focuses on helping you develop new strategies for managing the narcissist in your life. You are probably eager to get started, since the strategies that you've used before have not worked very well. But before you go any further, it's important to have realistic expectations of what you can and cannot change.

THINGS YOU CANNOT CHANGE

First off, what you are least likely to change is the narcissist himself. You shouldn't expect the narcissist in your life to change for your sake, and for a number of reasons, narcissists are typically unlikely to change on their own.

Narcissists Do Not Understand They Are Narcissists

One of the reasons that narcissists are unlikely to change is that they don't understand they are narcissists. They lack self-insight. They don't see themselves the way others see them, and they don't understand how disturbing their behaviors are to others.

It's widely accepted that teenagers will often behave narcissistically and that the teen years may be a trying time for parents. Luckily, most teenagers outgrow their narcissistic behavior as they begin to develop a deeper sense of empathy for others. Those who don't, however, will become adults who have the same sense of self-entitlement and lack of empathy. A narcissist may feel he is being empathic by stepping over the homeless person on the sidewalk and not stepping on him. Similarly, if you ask a narcissist to change a behavior that bothers you, he will lack the empathy to respond constructively.

Note that someone with full-blown NPD is going to be more difficult and resistant to change than someone who displays only intermittent episodes of egocentric behavior. Luckily, the strategies in this workbook can be applied to anyone who displays narcissistic traits.

Lack of self-insight is a trait that people with personality disorders have in common, and it's a problem that all narcissists share, to a greater or lesser extent. This lack of insight only serves to fuel the narcissistic behavior. There may be moments where a narcissist comes face-to-face with his behavior, but these moments are fleeting. Such a moment of truth was well-portrayed in a *Seinfeld* episode in which George Costanza attends a child's birthday party given by the woman he is dating. At one point, the stove in the apartment catches on fire, and George pushes all the children, the other adults, and even the child's grandmother out of the way so that he can save his own skin (a truly narcissistic behavior). When questioned by the firemen as to what took place and why he was the first one out of the apartment, George launches into a lengthy rationalization about how it was his responsibility to "lead the way" for the others to escape. At this point, the clown who was providing the entertainment for the children's party turns to George and says, "Man, how do you live with yourself?" and George responds, "It's not easy." Moments of such insight are usually rare in the life of a narcissist. Instead, the narcissist is usually well defended, and self-insight is missing.

Narcissists Are Unlikely to Change

Another characteristic common to all personality disorders that makes change difficult for the narcissist is that these personality traits are often of a long-standing nature and are therefore neither transient nor easily changed. Imagine changing from being right-handed to left-handed. Imagine if you were a political conservative all your adult life and then tried to change to become a liberal (or vice versa). So too, for the narcissist, it's almost incomprehensible to envision change. Neither would she see the necessity for change. For example, in the aftermath of a relationship breakup or even a marital separation, a narcissist would probably enter counseling only if court ordered or forced into it and, even then, would likely present herself as the victim or injured party, as if to say, "How could he or she have done this to me?" The narcissist is unlikely to enter counseling to examine how her behavior may have contributed to the relationship's demise.

Why Therapy or Counseling May Not Help

Did you ever hear the old joke "How many therapists does it take to change a lightbulb?" Answer: "One, but the lightbulb must really want to change."

Psychotherapy and counseling are effective for people who truly want to change. Truth be told, therapy is less effective or ineffective with people who want no part of change, and this is as true for narcissists as it is for anyone entering counseling. In instances where people are court mandated into psychotherapy or counseling, it seems the best we can do as counselors is to whet their appetite for change or try to tip the balance for those who may be ambivalent about change. Some people truly have to hit bottom before they will even begin to consider the notion that it's they who need to change, not those around them. This difficulty is commonly seen with alcoholics and drug addicts, who often must hit bottom before they can begin to see that it is their drinking or use of drugs that's creating the problems in their lives and relationships.

It's commonly believed that counseling alone will remedy any self-absorbed and egocentric behavior. Parents often feel that if they can just get their belligerent teenager to go for counseling, she will be able to talk out her anger. Similarly, many spouses of narcissists believe that if they can just get their mate to go to counseling, it will turn him into a compassionate, empathic human being. Here's the glitch: the narcissist must be a willing participant in the process of therapy or counseling in order for it to work.

A partner's willingness to enter counseling can be a positive step, but if that partner is not genuinely interested in change, he won't change. For example, it is an accepted practice not to treat couples when battering is present in the relationship. The reason is that the batterer will often use things the partner reveals in counseling as a further excuse to batter. We also don't mean to imply that all narcissists are evil, cruel, and calculating. The point is that therapeutic change begins with motivation and a willingness to confront uncomfortable things about oneself. Unfortunately, narcissism often works against the narcissist when it comes to truly benefiting from therapy, as is illustrated in the following case.

◆ Charles's Story

Charles sought out counseling at the advice of his secretary because of problems he was having in his five-year relationship with Susan. Charles's secretary had become tired of hearing about all his problems, the constant breakups and reconciliations. Charles was basically a user, and this was evident in how he treated his staff and how he treated Susan. It seemed that his relationship with Susan would go along fine as long as Susan did precisely what Charles wanted. At one point, Charles broke up with Susan because she wanted to spend time with her brother over the holidays and refused to stay home with Charles, who only wanted to watch football. Another time Charles broke up with Susan because she took too long to get ready when they were going out for dinner. None of these issues ever got resolved because Charles always felt that he was right and Susan was wrong or being unreasonable. For the first few months of couples counseling, Charles worked tirelessly trying to convince the therapist to agree with him that Susan was being unreasonable. Charles was unable to see his role in these arguments or to consider Susan's point of view. It took a lot of skill and a great deal of patience on the therapist's part to help Charles view these issues from Susan's perspective rather than just his own. However, Charles would only do this begrudgingly as a means of getting Susan to come back to him.

In many instances, those living or working with narcissists will take the approach that if they are patient enough or loving enough or smart enough, they will be able to change the narcissist or that they will eventually win the narcissist's love or approval. Unfortunately, it doesn't work that way.

It's also understandable how you can get caught up in what we call "the Ebenezer Scrooge myth." In the story of Dickens's *A Christmas Carol*, Ebenezer Scrooge goes through an incredible transformation from being nasty and miserly to affable and generous over the course of one night after being visited by the spirits of Christmas Past, Present, and Future. What is so appealing about this story is that Scrooge is able to make a miraculous change after seeing himself from a different perspective. Many believe that therapy works in this way, that if the therapist is skilled enough and smart enough, a miraculous change will occur. In some instances, miraculous changes in therapy are possible; this is most evident with alcoholics and addicts who go through an amazing transformation when they truly embrace recovery. By and large, however, such changes, whether they be with narcissists or addicts, are unfortunately few and far between and are rarely as dramatic as what Dickens portrayed. Instead, the work of therapy is often a lengthy and arduous process.

Exercise: Looking at Your Expectations

Check off any of the following statements that may apply to you:

☐ 1. You sometimes think that you can change the narcissist.

☐ 2. You have tried to change the narcissist's behavior or attitudes.

☐ 3. You believe that you can change the narcissist's behavior or attitudes.

☐ 4. You believe that if you love the narcissist enough, he or she will change.

☐ 5. You believe that if you accept the narcissist, he or she will change.

☐ 6. You believe that the narcissist is capable of change and eventually will change.

☐ 7. You believe that the narcissist will grow out of how he or she is.

☐ 8. You believe that if you do exactly what the narcissist wants, you can win his or her love or approval.

Take a look at the statements that you checked off. What does this list tell you about yourself and how you've been approaching your narcissist? Again, many people believe that if only they can figure out the right thing to say or do, the narcissist in their lives will change. We began to call this "the pork chop theory" after we heard the following story.

◆ Jim's Story

Jim was a twenty-eight-year-old who was referred to the local mental health counseling center by the courts. Jim was unemployed and had been living in the basement of his mother's home since he'd dropped out of his classes at the local community college. Jim had never held a steady job. He worked intermittently during the summer helping a friend of his who owned a landscaping business. Other than that, Jim would browbeat his mother when he needed money for cigarettes or to go out to a bar. In one incident, when his mother refused to give him money, Jim began smashing things around the house, and a neighbor called the police. One afternoon, Jim's mother called the counseling center and left a message for Jim's counselor that he had threatened to hit her if she didn't give him money to go out with his friends. She explained that she couldn't understand Jim's outburst given that she had just cooked his favorite pork chop dinner.

Jim's mother was operating under the belief that if she did nice things for Jim (like cooking him his favorite dinner), he would reciprocate by being nice to her and not demanding more money or threatening her. The problem with this reasoning is that Jim was incapable of reciprocity. It's tempting to believe that by being nice to narcissists or by placating them, they will be kind or compassionate in return. However, many narcissists, and especially those with NPD, are often incapable of reciprocity. In a similar vein, it would be unreasonable to expect a narcissist to take care of you physically or emotionally when you're hurting or to view your needs as being worthy of the her attention.

Hopefully, you've reached the conclusion that it's impossible to change other people and that you can only change yourself. However, it's normal to want to change others, especially the narcissist in your life.

Exercise: How Have You Attempted to Change the Narcissist in Your Life?

Below are three columns. In the first column, make a list of all those things you've wished your narcissist would change about himself or herself. In the second column, write down the things you did to try to change or to motivate your narcissist to change (such as nagging, threatening, rewarding, punishing, or giving ultimatums). Then in the third column, write down the outcome.

Change You Wanted	Things You Tried	Outcome

It is not unusual for people who aren't narcissistic to feel responsible for changing the narcissist in their life, and they will go to great lengths to try to bring about positive changes. It's normal to think that with a lot of effort, care, or love, you will be able to bring about the changes you've wanted or dreamed about.

Indeed, there may be times when your narcissist does seem responsive, when he does pay attention to your needs, or when she does make you feel special. These rewards may inspire you to continue trying to change the narcissist. Again, we're not saying that all narcissists are evil, horrible people who set out every day to make your life miserable. Many have admirable qualities. The final exercise in this section will let you look at what you admire about the narcissist.

Exercise: What Do You Admire About the Narcissist?

Think about some of the things you may admire about the narcissist. List some of those traits, characteristics, or behaviors. Also think of recent situations in which he or she may have done something you appreciated.

_____

_____

_____

_____

_____

_____

_____

_____

Look over your list. It is precisely these admirable traits and positive situations that often make it more difficult for you to realistically assess your relationship and the likelihood that the narcissist in your life is capable of change.

THINGS YOU CAN CHANGE

The key to improving your relationship with the narcissist is to look at what you can change about your own reactions. You can do the following: shed your denial about the narcissist and how he affects you; stop thinking that the narcissist's behavior is about you; detach with love; and take better care of yourself.

Shed Your Denial

It's common for people who are dealing with narcissists to be taken in by their charisma, their charm, their seemingly high self-confidence and high self-esteem, and their ability to work the crowd. In other words, it's easy to be in denial as to what you're dealing with. We knew of a narcissistic physician who acted one way with his patients, another way with his office staff, a totally different way with colleagues, and yet a totally different way with his family. Most of his patients loved him and would sing his praises, although there were a few patients who saw beneath his veneer of caring and empathy and saw him more as a windbag who only wanted to talk about himself, his exotic scuba diving trips, and golf vacations. The patients who loved him also felt that this physician was there for them when they had a problem or an emergency. His office staff basically hated him. He treated them abusively and yelled at them for minor mistakes (which were often his own). Although some of his colleagues saw him as a highly competent physician, most of his colleagues disliked his constant one-upmanship; they disliked that he always had to be right or get the last word in a debate or argument. Many colleagues would refuse to refer patients to him for this very reason, yet some of the nursing staff felt he could walk on water and praised him for his caring bedside manner. His wife and kids saw him as an absentee husband and father who took a "do as I say, not as I do" approach to most situations.

So you can see how easy it is to be in denial about the narcissist, depending on what type of contact you have with this person or how involved you are with his life. It's important to recognize the narcissist for who he is. Once you do this, you will be in a better position to evaluate what you need and what you are not getting in the relationship.

Understand That Narcissism Is Not About You

Again, many people get caught in the trap of thinking that they are to blame for the narcissist's behavior or inability to love others. They may subscribe to the belief that if they loved her more, or if they did exactly what he wanted, the narcissist would eventually come around and be able to love or be there for them. The point is worth repeating:

You didn't cause it.

You can't change it.

You can't control it.

Once you grasp this, you will have made a major change in your approach to the narcissistic behavior.

Remember, though, that narcissists are quite adept at pushing blame for their behavior onto others. Given their hidden low self-esteem, they have difficulty accepting responsibility when things go wrong or don't go precisely as they planned. You have to be vigilant about not blaming yourself when the narcissist tries to blame you.

Detach with Love

Detaching with love is a concept that originated in Al-Anon: that you could detach from an alcoholic's behavior and attitudes while not shutting the person out completely or shutting off your love for him. Detachment is naturally much more difficult to carry out in daily life than it sounds. First you must be able and willing to identify narcissistic behavior in the other person (such as when she is acting arrogant, haughty, or entitled, or is demanding special treatment or attention). Second, you must be able to accept that these behaviors and attitudes are part of narcissism. Third, you must be willing to accept the fact that this is part of the narcissist's nature. This would be similar to the spouse of an alcoholic who instead of trying to figure out why the alcoholic just went on a three-day binge would accept that this is what alcoholics do: they drink.

Since detachment is easier said than done, it may be useful to provide you with a few examples of what detachment from a narcissist might sound like. Here are some sample dialogues, starting with what a narcissist might say to you and followed by how you might respond in a more detached way.

Narcissist: Can't you do anything right? I'm always stuck doing everything around here!

You: I guess you're right, I'm not perfect.

Narcissist: *(Talks while standing in line at a restaurant.)* I can't believe we're not being seated right away. Didn't you make the reservations?

You: Yes, I made them for 7:00 p.m. Maybe you should make the reservations next time instead of me.

Narcissist: I can't believe we're lost again. It's your fault!

You: I don't feel I'm to blame. Let's stop someplace so you can ask for directions from someone.

Narcissist: You always take too long to get ready when we go out. I've had it.

You: Maybe you should go on ahead of me since you're ready, and I'll meet you there.

Narcissist: You should give me the $100 so I can go out with my friends. You owe it to me.

You: Sorry. I don't have the money to loan to you right now.

Exercise: Practicing Detachment

Now take some examples from your own life. What are some things the narcissist might say to you, and how you might respond in a more detached way?

Narcissist: _____

Your response: _____

_____

Narcissist: _____

Your response: _____

_____

_____

In staying detached, you're neither accepting the blame that the narcissist may be trying to heap on you nor reacting defensively. The detached person, in effect, is saying, "Since you believe you're always right and I'm always wrong, there's really no point in arguing with you, is there?" Detaching with love doesn't mean you have to become robotic and unfeeling or uncaring; it simply means that you're no longer reacting to narcissistic behavior or attitudes.

Take Better Care of Yourself

Most people who are in the clutches of a narcissist often find themselves waiting for some payoff that never seems to be forthcoming. Narcissists are more often so absorbed with themselves and their own agendas that they never seem to get around to making good on commitments. Whether it be the narcissistic boss who promises his employee a raise or the narcissistic parent who promises to show up at her child's school play or the narcissistic friend who doesn't show up for a lunch date, the theme is similar: the narcissist fails to deliver.

You can't make the narcissist come through for you, but what you can do is take better care of yourself. An employee working for a narcissistic boss learns to take care of herself or to get her needs met elsewhere. Kids who grow up with a narcissistic parent learn to find other adults they can count on. Having a friend who is a narcissist is often like not having a friend at all. Taking better care of yourself can begin with a lowering of your expectations of this person.

You can begin to take better care of yourself by looking at other ways to get your needs met. Who are the people you can count on? Are there ways you can treat yourself better rather than continue to expect something that your narcissist may not be able or willing to give?

Exercise: Treating Yourself Better

Make a list of people in your life who you feel you can count on:

_____

_____

_____

Now make a list of things you can do to treat yourself better or ways to get your needs met without having to rely on the narcissist in your life:

_____

_____

_____

_____

_____

_____

Great job! You've just begun to emancipate yourself from narcissistic behavior.

LOWERED EXPECTATIONS OR REASONABLE EXPECTATIONS?

You've probably heard the colloquial definition of insanity: when you do the same thing but expect a different result. It may be nuts to expect a narcissist to change when the result is always disappointment, but this is all too often what people close to a narcissist continue to do. It's easy to get caught up in the expectation that the narcissist can be different or that he will change. As discussed earlier, this is partially due to the fact that at times a narcissist will seem to muster some degree of empathy or warmth or what appear to be loving feelings, but usually these moments either are short-lived or represent feigned behaviors.

As you embark on the challenge of changing yourself and your approach to the narcissist in your life, here are some recommendations for keeping things in perspective:

1. Don't expect the narcissist to change.

2. Don't expect genuine warmth or love from the narcissist.

3. Don't expect praise or appreciation from the narcissist.

4. Don't expect the narcissist to support you (especially in times of need) or to support your progress.

5. Expect that the narcissist will try to take advantage of you or exploit you.

6. Expect your narcissist to go to any lengths to build herself up, even if it means belittling you, criticizing you, or putting you down.

7. Expect the narcissist to assume you will treat him as special or unique.

As you contemplate these recommendations, consider whether you will be able to apply each in your daily life. The exercise that follows will help you examine what you can or cannot change.

Exercise: Assessing Your Expectations

The following seven questions will help you to better understand your expectations regarding the previous seven recommendations.

1. What would it mean to let go of the idea that the narcissist might be willing or able to change?

_____

_____

2. What would it be like for you to accept the notion that the narcissist may not be capable of genuine warmth or love? (Remember, narcissists are often unable to love others.)

_____

_____

3. What would it be like for you to continue to go without praise or appreciation from the narcissist? (Remember, no matter how much you do, or how well you do it, the narcissist will take you for granted.)

_____

_____

4. What would it be like for you to accept the idea that your narcissist will ignore your needs (especially during times when you are hurting) and won't support your progress or growth? (Remember, for narcissists it only matters if it's about their goals.)

_____

_____

5. What would it be like for you to refuse to be taken advantage of or exploited by the narcissist? (Remember, narcissists see nothing wrong with taking advantage of others. They feel entitled to do so.)

_____

_____

6. What would it be like to refuse to be belittled, criticized, or put down by the narcissist? (Remember, narcissists often struggle with their own feelings of inferiority, so disparaging you may be an attempt by the narcissist to build up himself or herself.)

_____

_____

7. What would it be like to treat yourself as special or unique? (Remember, narcissists often expect a great deal from others, and when what they expect is not forthcoming, they can get very angry and resentful.)

_____

_____

This exercise can tell you a lot about the changes you may or may not be able and willing to make. Do you need to lower your expectations or develop a set of more appropriate expectations based upon what you can and cannot change? Think about it.

══

Change happens gradually. It may be hard to see the positive results of your efforts right away. Sometimes it can help to visualize how change may look in the future. Doing so can help you see how things will be different and how differently you will feel in response to the changes that you are making.

══

Exercise: Visualizing Change by Letting Go

Read through the following visualization and then close your eyes and imagine yourself in the picture described. You may want to read aloud slowly while recording yourself and then play back the recording with your eyes closed.

Imagine you're walking along the beach on a beautiful day. It's sunny, there's a nice breeze, and the sun feels good on your face. The ocean air is refreshing and you stop to listen to the waves that gently lap up onto the shore. Now begin to think about all those things that your narcissist does that bother you. Allow yourself to feel any painful feelings that arise. Now imagine that you are releasing these painful or annoying behaviors, realizing that you were not the one who caused these problems or behaviors and that you cannot change these behaviors or traits. Instead what you've decided to do is to let them go. Imagine you've written down all these annoying or painful things and you're now putting them in a bottle and letting the bottle drift out to sea. You're letting go and now can begin to feel peaceful again.

It's important to realize that you can face painful feelings about your relationship and that you can cast these feelings adrift when you need to. This exercise may be used more than once to help you let go of any painful or angry feelings you may experience.

Visualizing Change Using the Miracle Question

The late Insoo Kim Berg, a pioneer in the school of therapy known as solution-focused therapy, would often ask her clients what she referred to as "the miracle question" (Miller and Berg 1995). She would ask her clients to imagine that if a miracle were to occur so that overnight they would be somehow changed in such a way that all their problems would be resolved, how would they know that the miracle had occurred? How would they be different? The following story shows how you can use this concept.

◆ Bill's Story

Bill and Carol had been living together for four years. Bill had reached a point where he felt he could no longer tolerate Carol's self-centeredness and insensitivity. He would find himself feeling angry and frustrated, and he dreaded coming home from work each night because Carol would usually meet him at the door with a list of complaints about things he'd done or failed to do. Bill felt that Carol's demands were unreasonable and that everything always had to be her way. Bill decided to seek counseling so that he could change how he was reacting to Carol's complaints and demands. The counselor asked Bill to close his eyes and imagine that a miracle would take place when he went to bed the following night. He was to imagine that when he woke up in the morning, he would no longer find himself feeling angry and frustrated with Carol, no matter what she said. The therapist then asked Bill, "How would you know that this miracle had occurred? How would you feel different? What would you do differently?" Bill thought about the question and at first hesitated. He then said, "If a miracle really occurred, I'd wake up feeling calm and relaxed, knowing that I no longer was focused on what Carol's demands, complaints, or criticism were. Let her complain all she wants."

The miracle question allowed Bill to begin to see what the solution to the problem would look like; in other words, how things would be different if the problem no longer existed. From what Bill described, if a miracle were to take place, he would feel calm and relaxed because he would have detached from Carol's unreasonable demands.

There are two really important aspects to the miracle question. First, it allows you to begin to look at the solution to the problem and explore how things could be different for you in the future. Second, it encourages you to examine how you could change in the future. In the example above, it is Bill who changes his response to Carol, and not Carol who miraculously changes.

You can't truly expect to change overnight, but visualizing how such solutions would appear can help you take the next steps to improving your life.

A RAY OF HOPE: CORRECTIVE LIFE EXPERIENCES

We don't want to paint the hopeless picture that all narcissists are incapable of change and will go through life always using people, exploiting others, and leaving a trail of broken hearts, destroyed careers, and dysfunctional family relationships. At the same time, we don't want to create confusion, since we've stressed that it's often impossible for narcissists to change. However, noted psychiatrist Elsa Ronningstam (2005) emphasizes the importance of "corrective life experiences," which can sometimes transform narcissists into compassionate human beings. These life experiences include corrective achievements, corrective interpersonal relationships, and corrective disillusionment.

Corrective achievements are real accomplishments that seem to provide narcissists with the type of self-validation that they lacked as children or adolescents. This might include receiving a promotion, attaining an academic degree, or achieving an award or some other recognition. Once some narcissists attain such goals, they are able to let go of the need for constant praise or recognition and no longer need to be the center of the universe.

Corrective relationships may also bring about this transformation. These relationships are usually committed, long-term relationships in which the narcissist's sense of specialness or entitlement is replaced with a willingness to accept a partner for who she is rather than for what she can do for the narcissist. These relationships are characterized by mutual respect and caring. The potential for empathic communication in these relationships often allows the narcissist to begin to explore emotions from his partner's perspective.

Corrective disillusionment occurs when the narcissist is presented with some hard life lessons that take him down a peg or two. This can include the loss of a love relationship, the loss of a job or career, or a financial loss. In these instances, the narcissist realizes that he has no one to blame but himself. Although you cannot conjure up corrective life experiences, you can provide corrective communications and can model a corrective interpersonal relationship for your narcissist. We will talk about this in greater depth in chapter 7, on communication.

CHAPTER 6

Setting Limits and Boundaries

One of the problems that most people encounter when dealing with narcissists is that they can often be so unreasonable and unjust. From the narcissist's perspective, the world should revolve exclusively around him. This chapter presents some ideas on how you can begin to set limits on the narcissist's behavior and establish better personal boundaries.

At times it may feel like the narcissist has taken over your every waking moment or envelops your every thought and emotion. Remember, a true narcissist is extremely good at portraying himself as being the center of the universe; he is really good at making you feel that your purpose in life is to serve him. Why? Because he truly believes that he is so incredibly unique, talented, and special and that you are not. What's often amazing is how once his power is taken away, or he is exposed or disarmed, he no longer seems to have the same hold over others. This is often true of schoolyard bullies. As long as their peers quake in fear as the bully approaches, he will have incredible power over his classmates, but as soon as someone stands up to him, the tide changes rather quickly. Remember the scene from the movie *A Christmas Story* where Ralphie finally stands up to the school bully and bloodies his nose? We're not suggesting that you wrestle your narcissist to the ground and start pummeling him (however tempting this may be). Instead, what we will have you explore are ways in which you can stand up to the narcissist, so you are no longer bullied into doing things that you really don't want to do or that you may feel obligated to do.

VALUING YOURSELF AND INCREASING YOUR SELF-WORTH

One of the starting points for setting limits and boundaries is being able to accept that you have rights too. It's easy to feel that you don't count or don't matter if you've been dealing with a narcissist for any appreciable length of time. After a while, you may get brainwashed into thinking that the narcissist is the only one who matters and that you are just along for the ride. Jan Black and Greg Enns (1997) make the point that boundary setting is not so much a matter of mastering special techniques or catchy phrases to use as it is a matter of putting into practice a feeling of how you should be treated.

Chapter 5 concentrated largely on what you cannot change about the narcissist in your life. What you can change in your life begins with your self-worth. Valuing yourself and creating a greater sense of your own worth won't happen magically but rather will come from practice and concerted effort. Remember, it's okay to put yourself first.

How to Boost Your Self-Worth

Jan Black and Greg Enns (1997) list several ways to value yourself more. The following list is an adaptation of some of their suggestions:

◆ Make choices that are about you, choices that will affirm your self-worth, such as doing more activities that are self-affirming.

◆ Acknowledge your fears and what causes you anxiety, but try to challenge these fears. Don't let them get the best of you. For example, if you're anxious about flying, try to challenge your fear by flying to a place you will enjoy or have never been to before.

◆ Acknowledge your preferences, whether they be eating certain foods or doing certain leisure activities, such as going to the movies, pursuing artistic hobbies, or reading books, and plan time to enjoy what you like.

◆ Decorate your home, apartment, condo, or office in ways that you find pleasing. Use photos or pictures that are your own and that help to assert that this is your space.

◆ When you're having a difficult time making decisions, pretend you're offering advice to a friend of yours. What would you suggest to your friend?

◆ Visualize your goals. Where would you like to be a month from now, three months from now, six months, or a year? Visualize how you will be and how you will be different.

As you review this list, could you imagine yourself following through with some of these actions? Which do you feel would be easier for you to accomplish? Which would be more difficult for you? If some actions seem like they would be more difficult, it would be helpful to examine what you feel may hold you back.

Exercise: Taking Time for Yourself

Check off which of the following activities you will commit to start doing regularly. Indicate whether you will do them on a daily, weekly, or monthly basis by adding the letter D, W, or M (for daily, weekly, or monthly) in the blank next to the activities that you choose:

☐ Take time before going to work to read the newspaper or a magazine.

☐ Take some time before work to exercise or go for a walk.

☐ Take some time in the morning to have coffee, tea, or even a full breakfast.

☐ Take some time in the morning to do some daily meditation.

☐ Pick up a book or magazine that is of interest to you and read it.

☐ Take some time to call a friend of yours.

☐ Plan to spend time with a friend of yours.

☐ Go to a movie, concert, or play that you want to attend.

☐ Watch a TV program that you find enjoyable or entertaining.

☐ Take time to do something physically active that you enjoy.

☐ Take time to listen to music that you enjoy.

☐ Schedule regular doctor and dentist appointments or any other appointments that help to improve your health and well-being.

☐ Eat at a restaurant where you want to go. If you have to go alone, bring a book to read.

You can add to this list with other ideas, such as signing up for a class on a subject that especially interests you or taking time on the way home from work or school for a special activity that you enjoy. Making a commitment to take more time for yourself will improve your self-worth.

EMPOWERING YOURSELF BY SETTING BOUNDARIES

Albert Bernstein (2001) provides some useful suggestions for setting boundaries with what he refers to as "narcissistic vampires." For example, Bernstein suggests that you ignore the narcissist's tantrums rather than react or respond to them. He also suggests that you pick both your words and your battles carefully but that it's better not to cave in to what the narcissist is demanding or let the narcissist walk all over you. Asserting yourself and asking that your needs be met will give you a better chance of being heard; at the very least, the narcissist may respect your willingness to stick up for yourself. Chapter 7 will talk more about getting the narcissist to hear you and how to get your point across.

You may want to take a minute to think of the types of situations where the narcissist in your life does things that really bother or annoy you. Does she make demeaning comments about you (about your appearance or something you like)? Does he always say things that are designed to draw attention to himself or does he boast about real or imagined achievements? Does she make jokes at your expense? Does he spend an inordinate amount of time on his own appearance? Is she insensitive to your needs? Is he totally oblivious to what you think or feel? If the narcissist is in your workplace, does this person take credit for your work? Does she exploit you for her own gain or well-being? Does he make unreasonable demands of your time or efforts?

In order to set limits on these behaviors, it's important that you begin to think of ways you can react that are different from how you may usually react. It just makes sense that "If you want to feel something you've never felt before, you must be willing to do something you've never done before." If what you've been doing isn't working, you will have to consider trying a different approach.

Learn to Say No

The first thing you'll need to do is add the word "no" to your vocabulary. If you have tried to set limits with the narcissist and were unsuccessful before, you will need to be patient. You can set limits if you are firm enough. Here are some examples of how to respond:

Narcissist: Could you take care of my pit bull for the weekend? I'm planning on going camping with my friends.

You: No!

Narcissist: I'm really short on cash. Could you loan me $200?

You: No!

Narcissist: I'd like you to come in to work over the weekend to get some reports done.

You: No, I can't. I've already made plans and will be away this weekend.

Narcissist: Could you take my mother to the doctor? I have another appointment.

You: No. I have an appointment that day as well.

Stick to Your Guns

One of the problems that you may encounter with the narcissist is that she won't take no for an answer. If you say no, most narcissists will only ratchet up their demands. So what do you do when this happens? Answer: Stick to your guns.

To expand on the previous examples, here's how you might respond:

Narcissist: Could you take care of my pit bull for the weekend? I'm planning on going camping with my friends.

You:	No!
Narcissist:	But if you don't watch Sparky, I'll have to cancel my plans. That's pretty selfish of you.
You:	Sorry, I'm busy this weekend, and I can't do it.
Narcissist:	I'm really short on cash. Could you loan me $200?
You:	No!
Narcissist:	But I have to pick up my prescription. Don't tell me you don't have a measly $200 to spare? I'll pay you back when I get my paycheck.
You:	No! I'm not loaning you any money.
Narcissist:	I'd like you to come in to work over the weekend and get some reports done.
You:	No, I can't. I've already made plans and will be away this weekend.
Narcissist:	This work really needs to get done. I guess I won't be able to recommend you for a bonus.
You:	I'm not coming in this weekend.
Narcissist:	Could you take my mother to the doctor? I have another appointment.
You:	No, I have an appointment that day as well.
Narcissist:	But I can't take her. You'll need to change your appointment.
You:	No, I'm busy that day.

It's important to remember that in sticking to your guns, you are simply restating what you've told the narcissist. There's no need to come up with an elaborate excuse. No means no! You really don't have to explain yourself, though sometimes it may be helpful to reinforce that you're unwilling or unable to do what's being asked of you. If you're having a hard time saying no, imagine if the situation were reversed: if the narcissist was refusing to do something that you've asked of him, would he provide you with an explanation? Think about it.

It's important not to give in to threats or intimidation (such as the threat of being denied a raise or recommendation). If you give an inch, the narcissist will take a yard. As Sandy Hotchkiss (2002) points out, the operative word when setting boundaries is *control*, meaning that you stay in control. Remember, narcissists are usually accustomed to being in control and getting others to do their bidding, so at first it may seem somewhat unusual for you to take control and set the boundaries.

Another way to set limits on narcissistic behavior is to identify those behaviors that you are no longer willing to tolerate. You can write a statement or declaration that you are no longer willing to tolerate these behaviors any longer. This personal declaration of independence is your statement of boundaries; it's not meant to be shared with anyone. Even more important than writing down what you will no longer tolerate is following through with it. Remember, actions speak louder than words.

Exercise: Your Declaration of Independence

Please fill in the blanks to create your own declaration of independence:

I, _____ , being of sound mind and body do hereby swear that I

will no longer tolerate or put up with the following behaviors: _____

_____

_____

And in instances when I encounter these behaviors, I will respond by _____

_____

_____

DIFFICULTIES WITH BOUNDARY SETTING

People who have difficulty accepting that they deserve better treatment often come from homes where they were treated poorly or abusively. If you have difficulty setting boundaries, the following exercise may help you find the origins of this difficulty.

Exercise: Where Did Your Difficulty with Boundary Setting Originate?

Answer each of the following questions on a scale of 1 to 3, where 1 means this never happened, 2 means this sometimes happened, and 3 means this happened a lot.

_____ 1. Did you feel that either of your parents invalidated your thoughts or feelings?

_____ 2. Were your parents verbally abusive to you (yelled or screamed at you or were critical of you)?

_____ 3. Were your parents physically abusive toward you (hit, punched, or kicked you)?

_____ 4. Were your parents neglectful of your needs? Did you not receive much love or nurturing while growing up?

_____ 5. Did your parents neglect your regular medical and dental checkups?

_____ 6. Were you ever physically or sexually abused by anyone when you were a child or adolescent?

_____ 7. Were you rejected by one or both of your parents?

_____ 8. Were you ridiculed, belittled, or made fun of as a child or adolescent?

_____ 9. Were you ever threatened with being sent away from your family (for example, your parents threatened to send you off to live with a relative or to a boarding school)?

_____ 10. Did you ever witness physical or sexual abuse of a family member while growing up?

Now add up your score. If you scored 10, then you probably grew up in a nonabusive environment in which your needs were addressed. If your score was between 20 and 30, then you probably grew up a home that was abusive or neglectful or at least invalidating. It is usually people who score in the latter range that have difficulty in setting boundaries with narcissists, for they have difficulty valuing and loving themselves.

There appear to be a couple of reasons why people who come from dysfunctional or abusive homes become attracted to narcissists and vice versa. If you grew up in a damaging home environment, healthy self-love is something that was probably never modeled or displayed. Therefore, when confronted with a narcissist who appears to exude self-confidence and self-entitlement, you may see that person as having all that you were not given as a child and feel you are lacking. This was described brilliantly in *Getting the Love You Want*, by Harville Hendrix (1988), who proposed that people generally tend to look to their partners to make up those missing pieces of their damaged selves that they experienced during childhood. This is especially true in love relationships, but it may occur in other types of relationships, such as work relationships or friendships, where the same dynamics are at play.

Hendrix asserts that it is no accident that we become attracted to the people we do. So it is perhaps no coincidence that certain types of people might find themselves in the clutches of a narcissist. Conversely, narcissists are often quite skilled at picking people whom they can dominate. Remember, however, that most narcissists also feel wounded and have learned to overcompensate by taking on the opposite persona. If you have difficulty setting boundaries, for whatever reason, remember that it is your right to set them, especially in stopping patterns of being treated abusively.

CHAPTER 7

Establishing Better Communication

Chances are you often walk away from an encounter with the narcissist, saying to yourself, "I feel like I may as well be talking to the wall." As a result of this type of frustration, you, like many others who interact with a narcissist on a daily basis, may tend to ignore the narcissist, become annoyed or outraged but say nothing, or find yourself exploding.

Narcissists are in love with the sound of their own voices, so they're usually not interested in hearing your views or having a meaningful dialogue. They would rather talk at you than with you. But before you get out the sledgehammer and start beating your narcissist over the head to get her attention, you may want to try applying the basic communication skills covered in this chapter. Although you're probably already familiar with these skills, it may be helpful to review some general guidelines and then examine how to apply them to narcissists.

Remember as you read this chapter that the most important thing is to try something different from what you've been doing. You may need to do several different experiments before you can determine what works and what doesn't.

COMMUNICATION SKILLS 101

Most people find it difficult to communicate angry or frustrated feelings, which is why they tend to bottle up feelings or explode. What's unfortunate is that neither option provides much relief or produces the results you're after. The alternative that seems to work best is to use an assertive response. You may also find it helpful to use humor or sarcasm, to be the grown-up in the situation, or to keep it real by modeling or reinforcing appropriate behavior or responses.

Be Assertive

When you are unhappy with another person's behavior, it's usually a good idea to express how you feel in response to that behavior. Starting a statement with how you feel about the behavior allows you to say what's on your mind without sounding judgmental. This way, the other person will be less likely to react defensively to what you say and be more likely to hear you. The following is a standard formula for being assertive:

1. Identify what it is you are feeling in the situation.

2. State that feeling with a simple "I felt _____ when you did _____."

3. Don't try to explain or justify your feelings. Feelings are neither right nor wrong; they are simply a statement of your internal experience.

4. Stick to your guns after making an assertive statement. Again, you don't have to justify how you feel.

5. Examine how you feel afterward. If you've been successful in making a good assertive statement, you won't be fuming (as you might be if you'd bottled up your feelings), nor will you feel guilty about simply stating how you feel.

Exercise: Practicing Being Assertive

The next time you're faced with a situation in which you're lying in bed at night tossing and turning because of some situation where you find yourself saying, "I should have said _____," think of an assertive statement you could have used to hit the mark without bottling up your feelings or blowing up at the other person.

◆ Sue's Story

James and Sue have been married for the past twelve years. Sue often complains to her friends that James has become more demanding over the years and must always have things his way. As an example, Sue made plans months ago to visit her brother and sister-in-law at their home in Phoenix. James was agreeable to the plans and said he would make sure the date was on his calendar. Sue went ahead and purchased plane tickets and booked their hotel reservations. Three days before they were supposed to fly out to Phoenix, however, James announced to Sue that he didn't "really feel like going" and "besides I'm really busy at work right now." Sue was infuriated but said nothing. She cancelled their plans and didn't speak to James for a week.

◆ *Vivian's Story*

Vivian works in the corporate offices of a women's clothing retail chain. For the past two years, she has been reporting to Beth, who came to the company after having worked as a buyer for a large department store. At first Vivian liked Beth and felt she could learn from her. As time went on, however, Vivian became more frustrated with Beth because of her temper tantrums and abusiveness. At first Vivian would let the demeaning remarks go but then would find herself feeling resentful and would have trouble falling asleep as she went over and over in her mind things she should have said. One day after having a very difficult week, Beth lashed out at Vivian about an expense report she had submitted, saying "it was written by a third-grader." Vivian couldn't take it anymore and told Beth that if she didn't like it, she could shove it.

In these stories, Sue bottles up her feelings, going along as if nothing happened while seething inside, while Vivian bottles up her resentments until she reaches a point where she blows up at Beth. Clearly, neither bottling up your feelings nor blowing up brings about any relief. It's likely that Sue walks around for weeks with major resentments, while Vivian finds herself feeling guilty about things she's said in the heat of anger and may even fear retaliation.

Being assertive is an alternative worth trying. But there's a caveat. Basic assertiveness may not work as well with narcissists as it does in other situations. Often when you confront a narcissist directly, he will become either defensive or angry and may even lash out at you, almost as if you had blown up or exploded at him. The reason is that narcissists will often take clear and direct assertive statements as an assault on their character or their sense of uniqueness or grandness. It's like the narcissist is saying, "How dare you attack the king?" So here's where you need to modify your assertive statements so that you don't walk into a buzz saw.

It's quite likely that you've already experienced what most do when dealing with narcissists: if you don't say no or set a boundary, he or she will walk all over you. In the following situations, however, the assertiveness formula has been modified to get the narcissist to see things from your perspective, as well as to convey that you are unwilling to give into the narcissist's definition of the situation or issue at hand. In doing so, you're hoping to shape more considerate or empathic responses in the narcissist or, at very least, to get her to hear you.

Each of the following three situations gives a general assertive response, followed by an assertive response designed especially for use with a narcissist. Note in these examples how you may have to forget about expressing your feelings about the narcissist's behavior. Try to think of these situations as if you were dealing with an angry child or teenager who's throwing a tantrum. You don't want to escalate the argument, but neither do you want to give in to the other person's demands, so you need to communicate in a way that the narcissist will hear you.

SITUATION ONE

Narcissist: "I can't believe you forgot to pick up my jacket at the dry cleaners. Now what am I supposed to wear to work? You idiot!"

Assertive response: "I really resent your calling me names. Perhaps you should pick up your own dry cleaning from now on."

Assertive response to narcissist: "I'm sorry I forgot to pick up your dry cleaning. I was really overwhelmed with things I had to do today, and it slipped my mind. Let's see if we can find you something else to wear today. Let's also try to work out a better schedule for who picks up the dry cleaning and when."

SITUATION TWO

Narcissist: "I need you to stay late and finish up the Jones file."

Assertive response: "I feel taken for granted when you ask me to stay like this at the last minute. I already have plans for this evening, and it's not convenient for me to stay late."

Assertive response to narcissist: "I see the dilemma you're in about getting the Jones file complete. Unfortunately, I'm already committed this evening, and I can't get out of it. Perhaps I can come in early tomorrow and work on it?"

SITUATION 3

Narcissist: "I don't care if you're busy right now. Go get me a cup of coffee."

Assertive response: "I dislike being given tasks that are not part of my job description."

Assertive response to narcissist: "I know how busy you are right now, but I have a lot of work to do as well, which I know is important to you. Which would you rather I do?"

The following exercise gives you an opportunity to practice responding assertively.

Exercise: Responding Assertively to the Narcissist

Consider which type of response (the more general assertive response or the assertive response to the narcissist) is more comfortable for you and appropriate in your situation. Then imagine how you would respond to each of the following statements:

Narcissist: "I'm not going to the movies with you tonight. I'd rather read the paper and watch TV."

Your response: _____

_____

_____

Narcissist: "I'm tired of cleaning up your messes. Can't you do anything right?"

Your response: _____

_____

_____

Narcissist: "I'm doing all the work around here. I can't believe I have to work with complete morons like you."

Your response: _____

_____

_____

Use Humor and Sarcasm

Different situations sometimes call for different responses. In some instances, assertive statements are more appropriate, but in other situations, you may find yourself being creative, using humor or sarcasm as a means to refrain from taking the narcissist's bait. Here are a couple of examples.

◆ *Diane's Story*

Joanne always likes to brag about all the men she's dated and how so many men are "naturally attracted" to her. Her friend Diane usually says nothing as Joanne goes on and on about her own sensuality. Usually when Joanne does this, she'll think nothing of making criticisms about Diane's weight or clothes.

Instead of responding to Joanne's remarks with silence, Diane could use humor or sarcasm to make a self-empowering statement. For example, if Joanne said, "I can't believe how Dave wouldn't take his eyes off me. I think he's really attracted to me," Diane could simply respond with "You know, Joanne, I really didn't notice. I guess what Dave does is not that important to me."

Here's another response: "You know, Joanne, you may be right. He did tell me he likes women with big butts."

Alternatively, Diane could say, "It must be wonderful to have so many men attracted to you. How do you stand all the attention?" Each of the above retorts is self-empowering for Diane.

◆ A Coworker's Story

Ted constantly boasts about how much money he makes, and whenever he's awarded a bonus, he can't resist telling everyone how big a bonus he received. His coworkers and friends are pretty fed up with his boasting. When Ted purchased a thirty-two-foot speedboat with twin high-performance engines, he couldn't hold himself back from showing pictures of it to anyone he could corner.

Ted's coworker might respond to Ted's bragging by saying, "You know that old expression, Ted, 'The larger the boat, the smaller the penis.'"

Another response might be "That is a nice boat, Ted. I just hope that the price of gas doesn't go up to over $4 a gallon again. I know this one guy who says that it costs him about $500 just to motor down the river and back."

Yet another response might be "That's really a great boat, Ted. You must have worked really hard, and it's good to know you're appreciated for what you do." Each of these responses is self-empowering.

Be the Grown-Up

There are many different ways to respond to narcissistic behaviors. The key is to be an adult, and you can always make that choice, according to the theory of transactional analysis (Harris 1967).

Transactional analysis posits that we all possess three ego states: the parent, the child, and the adult. When someone else makes critical remarks about you, she may be acting in the parental role (similar to when Joanne criticizes Diane's weight or choice of wardrobe). You have the choice of responding in the parent, the child, or the adult role. Responding as the parent, Diane would probably hurl a critical remark back at Joanne. Responding in the child role, she might throw a tantrum by yelling and screaming at Joanne or by sulking or crying. In the adult role, however, Diane takes Joanne's remarks in stride as she could by saying, "It must be wonderful to have so many men attracted to you."

The optimal level of communication, according to transactional analysis, is adult-to-adult communication. Unfortunately, when you are communicating with a narcissist, this optimal level of communication rarely happens. More often than not, the narcissist will come at you as either the harsh, critical parent or the petulant, demanding child. So your goal is to stay in the adult role, regardless of how you are approached.

Keep It Real

One way you can communicate effectively with narcissists is to model and reinforce appropriate behavior and responses. You can do this without bottling up or blowing up and actually respond to the narcissist as if he were just like everyone else. This can be done without inciting a defensive reaction or an attack. At the same time, you can keep your boundaries.

You can think of the following responses as sound bites to use in various situations with your narcissist. Remember, you're attempting to shape or model more positive, empathic behavior and trying to speak to the heart of what the narcissist really wants from you: your approval or admiration. These sound bites may be especially useful when the narcissist has been thoughtful, considerate, generous, or empathic. These are the types of behaviors you want to reinforce or acknowledge in some way.

- ◆ Sound bite: "I really appreciate it when you take my feelings into consideration."

- ◆ Sound bite: "You really can be very caring and considerate."

- ◆ Sound bite: "You have the ability to relate well to a variety of people."

- ◆ Sound bite: "I really like it when you compliment me or acknowledge my work."

- ◆ Sound bite: "It's really nice that you can be so generous."

Exercise: Using Sound Bites

Can you think of situations where you could have used one of these sound bites? List them below.

_____

_____

_____

_____

_____

DEALING WITH TIRADES AND TEMPER TANTRUMS

Some narcissists control others through temper tantrums. It's not uncommon to find this type of behavior when the narcissist feels cornered or fears that some mistake or inadequacy will be uncovered. In those situations, you can expect that the narcissist will launch into a tirade as a means of deflecting blame.

There are many possible ways to deal with narcissistic rage and tantrums. You will need to pick the strategy that best matches the type of narcissistic explosiveness you're dealing with. If you are dealing with someone who tends to escalate as he vents, techniques suggested by Albert J. Bernstein (2003) may be helpful:

- ◆ Try to understand the mind-set of the angry person.

- Speak softly; don't threaten or challenge the angry person.

- Determine what your goals are.

- Avoid trying to reason with the explosive person by using rational arguments or explanations.

- Ask for time to try to come up with a win-win solution.

- Create distance.

The strategies described above are best used with narcissists who throw tantrums or go into tirades rather easily. With a narcissist who is less prone to tantrums, you will be able to use some of the other assertiveness strategies discussed earlier in the chapter. Also, there's an old expression "You don't have to attend every fight you're invited to." So there are some situations, especially with volatile narcissists, where it may be better to simply walk away from the fight. It's better to pick your battles or to at least wait to respond until the narcissist will be more likely to hear you.

Keeping Yourself Safe

Some narcissists control others through physical abuse or threats of physical intimidation. If you find yourself in a situation where you are subject to physical abuse, violence, or threats of physical abuse, then it would be best to seek counseling immediately from an agency that deals with domestic or intimate partner violence.

Domestic violence encompasses not only spouse abuse but also abuse of elder parents, a teenage or adult child's abuse of a parent, a parent's abuse of a teenage or adult child, and physical violence among siblings. It can occur in any intimate relationship, including dating relationships and gay, lesbian, bisexual, or transsexual relationships.

While not all narcissists are physically abusive, most batterers and violent abusers tend to be narcissists. In our years of clinical experience in working with batterers, we have yet to come across a batterer who was not narcissistic. Most batterers come up with elaborate justifications for their abusiveness as a means of avoiding taking responsibility for their behavior. What most of these rationalizations and justifications have in common is that the batterer is essentially saying, "I am right and you are wrong" or "You pushed my buttons and made me hit you." This is an incredibly narcissistic perspective. Very rarely do you find batterers who express regret or remorse, and if they do, it's often to avoid abandonment or avoid criminal prosecution.

If you find yourself in a relationship that has the potential for violence, you will need to keep yourself safe and strategize about what you would do in an emergency. We cannot emphasize too strongly that the best course of action is to seek counseling. You should also take the following steps:

- Contact the domestic violence counseling centers and shelters that are available in your community and obtain telephone numbers for twenty-four-hour hotlines. The counselors at these centers often know which police officers in the community have had special training to deal with domestic violence. Obtain the phone numbers of your local police department and these trained police officers.

- Begin to put together an emergency kit (in the event you need to leave quickly). This kit would include credit cards, bank statements, your Social Security number, checkbooks, cash, ATM cards, mortgage or rent receipts, your medical insurance card, your address book, an extra set of car keys, and a list of emergency numbers. Keep this kit in a place where you could grab it quickly (in a closet near the door or even outside the home in a secure place that only you are aware of).

- Identify exits or escape routes from various places within your home.

- Open a savings account in your name only and have records of this account sent to a friend's home or to a post office box. Make regular deposits.

- Keep a journal of any instances of abusive behavior. Document any violent threats or instances of intimidation. Keep records of your counseling sessions or any medical treatment you receive.

- Give a friend, trusted family member, or neighbor a signal or code word that you will use if you are in trouble and need assistance and another code word to ask them to notify the police that you need immediate assistance. If there are children in the home, make sure they know how to dial 911 and can provide their name and address.

COMMUNICATING WITH EXPLOITATIVE NARCISSISTS

One of the hallmarks of narcissists is their ability to exploit others. This comes from their overwhelming sense of entitlement. From the narcissist's perspective, you were put on this earth to serve his needs. Therefore, you may often find yourself in situations where he will expect or demand that you do his bidding. In love relationships, family relationships, and friendships, the narcissist will think nothing of taking your car, your clothes, your money, or even your most prized possessions, without a thought for what those things might mean to you. In the workplace, narcissists exploit their coworkers, bosses, and subordinates just about every chance they get.

Each of the following dialogues gives a response that sets limits on the narcissist's exploitative behavior. The goal is to communicate that you're not allowing this type of behavior:

Narcissistic family member:	I'm taking the car. I have an important appointment that I need to get to.
You:	No you're not, I have plans this afternoon. I am willing to give you a ride to your appointment or give you bus fare. What's your choice?
Narcissistic coworker:	Could you punch the clock for me? I have to leave early today, and I don't want the boss to know.
You:	I'm not comfortable doing that. Besides, if I get caught, I'll get fired.

Narcissistic spouse/partner:	I'm taking $500 out of the checking account so I can buy a new fly fishing rod.
You:	No you're not. We need that money to pay off the credit card this month. Why don't you take the money out of your savings?

Exercise: Setting Limits on Exploitative Behavior

Imagine how you might deal with the following boundary violations. In each case, give a response that sets limits on the exploitative behavior:

Your narcissistic family member asks to borrow $400 to repair his car.

Your response: _____

_____

_____

Your narcissistic boss takes your work and presents it as if it were her own.

Your response: _____

_____

_____

Your narcissistic spouse or partner is out raking leaves in your sweatshirt because she doesn't want to get her own sweatshirt dirty.

Your response: _____

_____

_____

Your narcissistic friend says he hopes you don't mind that he has given your name as a cosigner on a loan he's applying for.

Your response: _____

_____

_____

Setting limits on exploitative behavior is not easy, but consider the alternative. Once you've opened the door to exploitation, the narcissist will expect he can continue to exploit you without consequence.

UNDERSTANDING YOUR REACTIONS TO THE NARCISSIST

Wendy Behary (2008) talks about three common reactions that people have to narcissistic behavior: the "fight, flight, and freeze" reactions. These reactions correspond to the responses to narcissists—angry/resentful, apathetic/detached, and denigrated/intimidated—that were presented in chapter 4. Those who feel angry or resentful are more likely to respond to the narcissist by fighting. Those who have become apathetic or detached are more likely to respond to the narcissist by flight. Those who are denigrated or intimidated are more likely to respond to the narcissist by freezing.

When you are choosing an alternative way of communicating with a narcissist, the best strategy is to decide what your response usually is (angry, apathetic, or denigrated) and then consider how to react differently.

SELECTING A COMMUNICATION STYLE

The following scenario with a narcissist could provoke an angry, apathetic, or denigrated response. As you read this story, think about how you would respond if you were in this situation.

◆ Ellen's Story

Ellen has worked for Dennis for the past two years as his administrative assistant. When she first started working for Dennis, she knew he was demanding; however, as time went on, she found that he was more and more abusive toward her. What made this situation worse was that Dennis would often berate Ellen in front of other coworkers in their group. Last Friday, just as everyone was getting ready to leave work, Dennis screamed at Ellen for not having the monthly report completed. In fact, the report wasn't due until the following Tuesday, and Ellen had planned to complete the report on Monday when she returned to work.

If you were Ellen, how would you respond? Consider the following alternatives to an angry/resentful, apathetic/detached, or denigrated/intimidated response.

Alternative to an Angry/Resentful Response

If Ellen were prone to becoming angry with Dennis, giving right back to him what he would dish out to her, than it might be helpful for her to try a different strategy. Ellen would first need to collect herself and be mindful of her goal in communicating with Dennis. She would then need to resolve that in talking with Dennis, she would not lose her sense of composure. After doing this, she might be able to have the following dialogue:

Ellen: Dennis, I'd like to talk with you about the monthly report. Do you have a minute to talk privately?

Dennis: Okay, but make it quick, I'm going skiing this weekend.

Ellen: Sure. First of all, I really don't appreciate being yelled at in front of my coworkers. I feel embarrassed and frustrated. The other thing is that I know the report isn't due until Tuesday, so my plan was to come in early on Monday and have it completed in plenty of time for you to review it. Have I been late with monthly reports before?

Dennis: No, but there's a first time for everything, Plus you were dragging around all day when you should have been working on the report.

Ellen: If you felt that way, you should have mentioned something earlier, and I would have worked on the report today. I've always gotten the reports done on time and will get this report in on time, and I'd appreciate it if you didn't talk to me the way you did.

In this scenario, Ellen is careful to keep calm, to stay in the adult role, and not to explode as she may have done in the past. By asking to speak with Dennis alone, she is modeling how she would like to be treated: "If you have something to say, say it to me privately, not in front of the others." She is also clear and direct in her communication.

Alternative to an Apathetic/Detached Response

If Ellen tended to react to Dennis's abusive comments by feeling apathetic or detached (avoiding the confrontation), we would recommend that she find some way to stand up to him and to stand up to his tirades. By sticking up for herself, Ellen is communicating that she will not tolerate abusive behavior:

Ellen: Dennis, I'd like to talk with you alone for a few minutes.

Dennis: Okay, but make it quick. I'm going skiing this weekend.

Ellen: Okay, I usually don't say anything in situations like this, but I wanted to let you know how angry I felt over you screaming at me in front of the others about the monthly report. I've never been late with these reports, and I feel that we've worked well as a team on these.

Dennis: Okay, is that all you wanted to talk with me about?

Ellen: Yes, that's it. Have a good weekend.

Here, Ellen is doing something she's not accustomed to doing: telling Dennis how she feels about his abusive comments. In the past, Ellen would have bottled up her feelings and spent the rest of the day in efforts to flee thoughts and feelings about the confrontation? She then would have had a miserable weekend as she obsessed over what she should have said if given the opportunity. So instead, she musters her courage, and her remarks are quick and to the point.

Alternative to a Denigrated/Intimidated Response

There may be times when you become overwhelmed by the narcissist as a result of her larger-than-life persona. If you find yourself feeling frozen or unable to respond, it can be helpful to have a fallback position. Here would be Ellen's alternative reaction if she felt this way:

Ellen: Dennis, I'm feeling a bit overwhelmed by your accusation about the report. I am working on the report and will have it to you by the deadline; however, I'd like to take some time to think about what just happened, and I'd like to talk about it some more on Monday.

Dennis: What's there to talk about? Just get the report in.

Ellen: I will get the report in, but I need to process what happened today, and I'd like to take some time to think it over.

Dennis: Okay. I still don't see what the big deal is.

Here, what Ellen is doing is buying some time to figure out what she is feeling and what she wants to say rather than shut down and go into freeze mode.

Again, you can choose how to communicate with the narcissist in your life. We hope that after reading this chapter you will be better equipped to deal with situations where your narcissist may be trying to exploit you or trying to steamroll you into his way of thinking or doing things. It's common when put in these situations to feel like the proverbial deer caught in the headlights, but with practice and persistence, you will be able to communicate more effectively and, in doing so, will be able to set more effective boundaries.

CHAPTER 8

Strategies for Managing Narcissists in Friendship, Love, and Family Life

By now you have most likely determined that you are in a one-way relationship with a very self-centered person. You have in all probability learned a good deal about your relationship. Most likely, you are considering making some changes. Are you willing to do things differently in your relationship with your loved one? This chapter will help you explore whether you are ready to make some important changes and will then give you some new strategies for managing the narcissist in your life.

DECIDING IF YOU ARE READY

Change almost always involves overcoming some of your own anxieties and taking risks involving your own personal growth. You will need to overcome your anxieties about change before you can begin to do things differently. You may ask yourself, "Are changes possible?" and "Should I make them?"

Now is the time to make some important choices. You will need to answer some tough questions.

Can You Forgive and Move Forward?

Forgiveness is the starting point. Most likely, your one-way relationship has hurt you in many ways, and you have needed to forgive your partner, friend, or relative in the past, but you will need to do it again. You cannot harbor resentment and maintain a good relationship; sooner or later, you will have to forgive the narcissist, and the sooner the better. Luckily, we are billionaires in forgiveness; we have an endless supply. Remember, you do not have to feel forgiving to forgive; it is an act of will, a decision you make, not a feeling. Also, forgiving does not mean foolishly assuming that the narcissist will do no more hurtful things in the future; he probably will and you should be on the alert so as not to be taken advantage of. It may be helpful to remember that forgiveness is also for you; by letting go, you can begin to heal too.

Exercise: Can You Forgive and Move Forward?

Are You Willing to Work on Just Yourself?

Another prerequisite for change is that you need to accept that you can only change yourself. Can you resist the temptation of trying to change the narcissist? It's easy to fall back into old patterns, especially when success is not immediate. And you may find yourself asking this: "Why do I have to change when she has the problem? Shouldn't it be fifty-fifty?" Quite frankly, we have never known a relationship to be fifty-fifty. And besides, making changes is empowering, because you are in control. Waiting around for others to change just makes you feel weak and angry. You may think it's unfair that you will have to do all the work now, since you're the only one who has worked for this relationship all along—after all, it's one-way! But most likely, you have worked in the wrong areas, especially if you have been trying to change the narcissist.

Exercise: Are You Willing to Work on Just Yourself?

Is Your Loved One Capable of Loving You the Way You Need to Be Loved?

To put it bluntly, would you bet on a horse that has never won a race? If the narcissist in your life has never had a successful reciprocal relationship, you are making this bet. Oh sure, the narcissist will claim to love you, but there are many types of love. A two-year-old loves his mother truly, but that is not the type of love you look for in a romantic partner or a friend. The narcissist's level of love is immature, but it is all that he knows. Can he grow in his level of maturity in loving? That is a tough one to call. Past success is a good predictor: Have you seen any maturation since you have known him? If so, there is hope.

Exercise: Can Your Loved One Love You the Way You Need to Be Loved?

Can You Settle for Half a Loaf?

They say that half a loaf is better than none. If you are to have a continuing and mutually beneficial relationship with the narcissist, you will probably have to put some of your expectations aside. For example, you might have to give up the idea that she will always be emotionally supportive of you or that she will take an interest in some of the things you love the most. You might have to take some of the things that you thought you'd do together and do them separately. The narcissist might never spend Christmas at your brother's or back you up in your arguments with your friends. But there may be other aspects of the relationship that will make it worth your effort.

Exercise: Can You Settle for Half a Loaf?

Are You Ready to Get the Help You Need?

You should seriously consider getting professional help in your one-way relationship. We recommend finding an expert who has a history of working with narcissistic clients.

Narcissists can be quite challenging for therapists, especially those who are not trained to work with them, so it's important to put some effort into finding someone with the right experience. A good resource might be a local university with a graduate program in clinical psychology, or you can try the Institute for Advanced Studies in Personality and Psychopathology in Port Jervis, New York, or the Personality Disorders Institute at Cornell University. Both institutes train clinicians to treat narcissistic people and may be able to recommend an expert in your area. (See resources for more information.) When contacting a professional, you will want to make an appointment for yourself; if the narcissist agrees to come, so much the better.

True friends and trusted family members can also be a good source of emotional support and encouragement, and you'll need them if you decide to make changes. There is also a good deal of reading material on narcissism, including information on the Internet. You will want to read all you can and become an expert. At the very least, you will know more about the topic than the narcissist in your life.

Exercise: Are You Ready to Get the Help You Need?

_____

_____

Have You Counted the Costs of Making Changes?

Making changes requires an investment of your time and energy. You should keep in mind that there is a sacrifice here. You will put in a good deal of effort before you see any results. In the beginning, you might have to endure some real trials, perhaps even a crisis. There is also the risk that your relationship will never get better, and you will have to confront this possibility if you decide to make changes.

Exercise: What Are the Costs of Making Changes?

Is There Enough to Build On?

Before you decide to make changes, you will want to explore if there's enough in your relationship to build on. This means asking yourself questions like the following: Have you seen areas of improvement in the past? Does your one-way relationship have some elements of reciprocity? Have you successfully negotiated anything in the past? Is your narcissist open to change? Has the narcissist responded to any of your needs in a consistent manner? Have you seen signs of commitment to the relationship? If not in your own relationship, has the narcissist demonstrated any of the above with others? Answering such questions in the affirmative means you have something to build on.

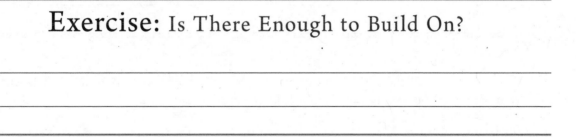

Exercise: Is There Enough to Build On?

Are You Too Afraid to Make Changes?

Unfortunately, many people fear changing what they do in a relationship. Perhaps they believe it is better to do the same old, same old, even if doing so is painful, because changing anything would risk losing the relationship. Here are some other common fears people have about changing their behavior in an unrewarding, one-way relationship:

- fear of criticism or ridicule

- fear of failure in a relationship

- fear of real intimacy or commitment

- fear of grieving the loss of a relationship

- fear of being alone

- fear of abandonment

- fear of confrontation

- fear of not having anything else to do with your life

Exercise: What Are You Afraid Of?

After asking yourself these important questions, you will know if you are ready to make changes in your relationship. If you are, then it's time to take the next critical steps.

CHOOSING WHAT TO CHANGE

Change can be understood as a three-step process in which you determine what changes you wish to make, you implement these changes, and you reap the rewards of your efforts. We will examine two different ways that you can change your relationship by changing what you do: the first is to maximize the positives and minimize the negatives with the narcissist; the second is to increase the amount of time you spend with the narcissist doing things that you both enjoy. We will also look at a third option on the cutting edge of therapy: using an intervention with the narcissist. There are no guarantees here, but with all of these methods, if you stick to your guns, you may be able to transform your relationship into more of a two-way reciprocal relationship with all of its attendant rewards.

Maximize the Positives

One of the most confusing aspects of a one-way relationship is that there can be some really good things in the relationship in spite of the negatives. This is one reason that many people find one-way relationships with friends or lovers worth working on. Or perhaps your relationship is with an ex, with whom you are required to coparent, or a family member. In these instances, leaving the relationship is not always possible. One way to change the relationship for the better is to minimize the negatives and maximize the positives, or detach from the fake and connect to what is real.

Detaching from the fake involves creating physical or psychological distance from the most troubling things about the narcissist. An instance of physical distancing could be telling your best friend that you do not want to go out to dinner with her this evening because she will be drinking too much. Psychological distancing, on the other hand, could be refusing to discuss your romantic relationship with a narcissistic parent who is critical of your romantic involvements. An important key in creating psychological distance is to recognize that there is a good chance that you yourself may be an issue: that you have something to prove, for example, that draws you into dysfunctional interactions. In the case just mentioned, you might have a need to prove to your parents that you are a competent person whose romantic choices are good. Giving up your desire to resolve your own personal issues through the narcissist goes a long way toward the creation of psychological space. It is a tactic that many people overlook.

But simply detaching from the fake, in and of itself, is not enough. Often the narcissist in your life will misinterpret this as a total rejection of the relationship. So just as it is important to detach, it is essential that you connect with the narcissist in an area of the relationship that you value: something that is real. So, to use the previous examples, detaching from the fake and connecting to what is real would go something like this: you would tell your friend that when she gets home from dinner, you would love to watch a movie with her, or you would say to your parents that you do not wish to discuss your personal relationships with them but you would like to stop by this weekend to help them with their spring cleaning.

What things should you connect to? Almost anything positive is good, but you should also try to connect to what is real (something you truly value) in the narcissist. It can be an exhilarating, liberating, and even therapeutic experience for a narcissist when he recognizes that—with all of his shortcomings and blemishes—his loved ones accept him for who he really is. He might even learn to seek out this acceptance instead of your admiration for his inflated self, of which he has spent a lifetime in pursuit.

Interestingly enough, the ancient Greeks in their myth of Narcissus were wise enough to include in their mythology that the spell cast on Narcissus to fall in love with himself could only be broken when he found out who he truly was! The same holds true for the narcissist in your life. Remember, his need to inflate himself only comes from his own belief that he is pathetic. Reaffirming what is real in the narcissist is an excellent way of affirming his worth, as you connect to what is real in him in a way that will not inflate his ego or tear him down.

The following exercise will help you figure out how to do this.

Exercise: Detaching from the Fake and Connecting to What Is Real

Create a list of things that the narcissist does from which you wish to detach. Start by checking off all of the following that apply in your situation:

- ☐ verbal attacks

- ☐ moodiness

- ☐ monopolizing the conversation

- ☐ negative statements about you and others

- ☐ efforts to control you

- ☐ blaming you for his or her mistakes

- ☐ threats of retribution

- ☐ temper tantrums

- ☐ bragging

- ☐ using you

- ☐ entitlement behaviors

- ☐ showing off

- ☐ use of alcohol or drugs

Now list some other things from which you would like to detach:

_____

_____

Next, list some things in the narcissist with which you wish to connect. Begin by checking off any of the following traits that you appreciate about the narcissist:

- ☐ enthusiasm

- ☐ desire for adventure

- ☐ hobbies

- ☐ excitement over a sports team

- ☐ love of cooking

- ☐ wanting to show you how to play golf or another sport or favorite game

- ☐ desire to travel

- ☐ love of videotaping the family

- ☐ fondness for old black-and-white movies

Now list some other traits that are worth reinforcing in the narcissist:

_____

_____

_____

After doing this exercise, you should be ready to change how you relate to the narcissist. The next step is to implement this change.

IMPLEMENTING DETACHMENT AND CONNECTION

How do you communicate your desire to detach from the fake and connect to what is real? Here's an example: Imagine you are coming home from work, and you wish to connect with your self-centered other by watching your favorite standup comedian on television that evening while enjoying some baked Alaska; both are activities you have previously enjoyed together. But when you come home, you find that your self-centered other just wishes to complain about how some family member of yours was too stupid to appreciate one of the narcissist's self-aggrandizing rants at the last family reunion. Your dialogue would go something like this:

Narcissist: How does that idiot brother of yours manage to keep his job? What a loser!

You: *(Detach from the fake and connect to what is real.)* Yeah. Hey, why don't I start the baked Alaska for tonight? Are you as excited as I am? Imagine, a two-hour special. I might not stop laughing until Thursday.

Narcissist: What? Are you defending him again? Are you as stupid as he is? I didn't think anyone could be.

You: *(Detach from the fake and connect to what is real.)* Seriously, it starts in about fifteen minutes. I have to start now if we're going to watch it on time. I got your favorite vanilla ice cream. Come on, you big Eskimo you, before I eat it all myself.

> *Narcissist:* (*Mumbles somewhat.*) Just stupid…can't understand anything…moron. Do you know what channel it's on?
>
> *You:* Now you're talking. I'm so glad that you turned me on to him. I love it that we have the same sense of humor. Five minutes to showtime!

Remember, you don't have to be nasty to be persistent. Notice in this imaginary dialogue that the connection was done lovingly and enthusiastically. Your goal is to refuse to fight.

This next exercise will prepare you to implement detachment and connection in your own one-way relationship. You'll find this to be a good way to defuse some of your relationship hot spots.

Exercise: Communicating Your Desire to Connect with What Is Real

Pick three situations with the narcissist in your life where you want to communicate your desire to connect with what is real, and then imagine what you would say in each situation.

1. Your narcissist is doing something you want to detach from. The narcissist does this by saying or doing the following:

   _____

   _____

   You respond by detaching from the fake and connecting to what is real in the following manner:

   _____

   _____

2. Your narcissist is doing something you want to detach from. He does this by saying or doing the following:

   _____

   _____

   You respond by detaching from the fake and connecting to what is real in the following manner:

   _____

   _____

3. Your narcissist is doing something you want to detach from. He does this by saying or doing the following:

_____

_____

You respond by detaching from the fake and connecting to what is real in the following manner:

_____

_____

Again, when you connect to what is real, you should be persistent and stick to your guns. Don't give up. Don't be lured into yet another hurtful interaction. Connection is an offer that a lot of people find impossible to refuse.

Find the Right Balance

As you choose what to change in your relationship, you may also want to look at how you tend to spend your time. Any type of relationship, be it friendship, romantic, or familial, can be seen as a balance between time that is totally for yourself and time that you spend together. An example of a "me activity" is spending time with your favorite niece apart from your loved one while he plays softball. Later on, you might join your partner in landscaping the yard, a "we activity." The balance of me activities to we activities is different in every relationship and is decided by the people involved; there is no right or wrong way. We all need to be by ourselves and do me activities because we are unique individuals who are different from the people we love. But we also need to do we activities when we are in a relationship. Problems arise in relationships when the two parties have different ideas of what is an ideal balance for them: some might like a relationship where they do 40 percent of their activities together and 60 percent apart, while others might like the reverse. People can falsely assume that their mix is the correct one. This is particularly true in romantic relationships.

It is our belief that conflicts arising over how much time you spend together and apart account for the greatest amount of fighting in one-way relationships and that a great deal of conflict can be resolved by renegotiating the issue. Here are some common related misconceptions known to cause conflict:

◆ "We have too many differences to have a relationship." This incredibly common but false assumption is based on the misconception that the two of you are the same. In actuality, there are hundreds of differences between you, ranging from which room temperature you feel comfortable with and how many hours of sleep you need to what your favorite foods and television shows are. You have different genes, had different upbringings, and may be of different genders. Irreconcilable differences can end relationships, yet every relationship begins with them.

◆ "She does not seem interested in anything I want to do." She doesn't have to be interested. There are thousands of things to do in this world. Find or create some things that you can do together.

◆ "If we are a couple, we should do everything together." No way! You have a need to grow individually and separately as well as to be together. Remember, you are different.

◆ "We just don't have enough in common." Then find something new. You may want to take a trip to the local bookstore and browse among the hundreds of books available on hobby, recreational, and travel ideas, for example. Websites abound for just about every interest known to mankind. You can use them to find some things you might like to do together.

Do you suffer from any of these misconceptions? The following exercise will help you correct some of the issues that may be causing problems in your one-way relationship. First you will identify your genuine differences. Next, you will list similarities and other things you may be able to build on.

Exercise: Me Time, We Time

Check off the areas in which you and the narcissist are different. Consider doing these things separately while connecting in other areas. This exercise is especially useful with romantic partners, but it can be applied to other relationships as well.

☐ You like different television programs.

☐ You have different friends.

☐ One of you does not get along with certain family members.

☐ You like different sports.

☐ You have different recreational desires.

☐ You like to eat at different times.

☐ You are of different faiths.

☐ Your political views are different.

☐ You like to go to bed at different times.

☐ You do chores differently.

☐ You have different interests.

What other things do you do differently?

_____

_____

Think of some things that you do together that you have both agreed should be shared activities. Check off any of the following that apply:

☐   cooking meals

☐   taking vacations

☐   eating out

☐   setting up child care

☐   spending time together during the holidays

What other things do you do together that fit into this category?

_____

_____

Finally, list some new things in which you feel you could connect and that would be relatively problem free.

☐   taking up a sport together, such as golf or skiing

☐   doing a hobby together, such as brewing beer or making home movies

☐   learning a new skill by taking classes in adult education

☐   doing some charitable work together for a worthy cause

☐   planning a trip

☐   starting a business

Now add some of your own ideas:

_____

_____

It should be obvious by now that narcissists are all about the "me time." One good strategy for avoiding fighting over their self-centeredness is to offer them their time to do things they want to do while making an invitation to do more things together. Here are some examples: "When you're done on the Internet, I thought that we could go out for some ice cream, okay?" Or "After you are done writing your speech today, would you like to go visit Amanda?"

Exercise: Making Me-Time, We-Time Statements

Acknowledge or promise the time the narcissist wants, and then ask for some time together. Use the following phrases to practice getting started.

1. "After you've had a chance to _____ ,

    how would you like to _____ ?"

2. "When you've finished _____ ,

    how about we _____ ?"

3. "I see that you're busy with _____ .

    When you're finished with that, can we _____ ?"

With more practice, it will become easier to acknowledge the narcissist's me time while asking for more we time. And you may just get the results you're looking for.

Do an Intervention with the Narcissist

It is a real challenge to make changes in a one-way relationship. Sometimes the best efforts fail. Perhaps there is one more option.

One of the newer, cutting-edge approaches being advocated by experts is the *intervention*. Doing an intervention can be a difficult yet valuable strategy in dealing with highly resistant narcissistic people. Interventions can take a good deal of time, preparation, and resources, and note that with intervention, you risk terminating the relationship. An intervention is a technique that was originally developed to break through the denial and resistance in a substance abuser who refuses to acknowledge her problem. Several key people in the substance abuser's life—family members, friends, and the like—confront her with her problem, the pain she has caused them, and their concern for her well-being. They are usually aided by a professional trained in interventions. In some instances, a bed in a rehab center has previously been reserved and the patient's bags are already packed.

More recently, interventions have been used to break through the denial of people with eating disorders. The fact that it is a technique specifically designed to prevail over denial makes it a good choice for narcissists because denial is one of their key symptoms.

We're aware that it may seem contradictory for us to propose intervention as an option with the narcissist, since we've emphasized throughout this book that the only person you can change is yourself. It's true that you can't make someone else change. The goal of an intervention, however, would be to break through the narcissist's denial, to help him see himself the way others see him. If it works, there is a strong possibility that the intervention would make the narcissist want to change himself.

Here are the steps in implementing an intervention:

1. Enlist the aid of a professional. Interventions can be very stormy and emotional experiences. While it is possible to have an intervention without a professional, your chances are better with the help of an experienced practitioner. One place to look is the Institute for Advanced Studies in Personality and Psychopathology (see resources).

2. Enlist your participants. These should be people who have some influence over the narcissist or people whom the narcissist has hurt in some way. Stick to about four or five people if you can.

3. Plan your intervention. The key participants should meet at least one time to plan the meeting without the narcissist's knowledge. In this meeting, you need to set goals, like getting the narcissist to commit to psychotherapy. Develop talking points; everyone should have only one or two key things to say. Try to stick to those points without hitting the narcissist with everything under the sun. Remember to communicate compassion throughout the session and resist the temptation to withhold it for revenge. Plan strategies for what to do if and when the narcissist resists. Be prepared to apply a consequence if the narcissist insists on carrying on the same old, same old. Ending the relationship, litigating, or not participating in certain activities with the narcissist are some possibilities. Leverage is your ace in the hole.

4. During the intervention, stay calm, for things can get rough. Remember, this is a loving gesture done out of concern. Make it clear that ignoring the problem would have only hurt the narcissist. You may be surprised that this show of support actually touches the narcissist. Avoid labels and general sweeping statements. Use I-messages. Stay upbeat and helpful.

Although interventions with substance abusers are generally effective, statistics on interventions with narcissists are not yet available.

IMPLEMENTING CHANGE AND REAPING THE REWARDS

Implementing changes will probably be difficult because you are trying to change the relationship in a new way that will not be familiar. Also, the narcissist will doubtless do everything in her power to make the relationship go back to the way it was. Most people tend to give up at this point, believing it is not worth the effort and that the old way was not as bad. They're wrong!

If you want to make changes in your relationship, you will need to be persistent. Changes come slowly in one-way relationships, and even small changes are good ones, especially in the beginning. Don't be disheartened if things in your relationship initially take a turn for the worse, for they almost always do, even in successful cases. Normal growth in relationships is usually two steps forward and one step back. Stick with it.

And don't overlook the professional help option, especially if you are considering ending the relationship. Every person and every relationship is different, and a professional will be able to utilize your unique strengths and abilities to find other solutions. A professional will also be able to help you move on should the relationship come to an end. And that is always an option as well.

CHAPTER 9

Strategies for Managing Narcissists in the Workplace

Narcissists at work present special challenges, but the difficulties depend most upon how much power, influence, and daily face-to-face contact exist. Thus, a narcissistic boss with whom you have constant contact will be a much greater challenge to you than a narcissistic coworker whom you rarely see. Because a good deal of your financial and emotional welfare depends upon your employment, destructive narcissistic relationships can be a little more critical than, for example, social relationships with the very self-centered. As a result, effective interactions can become even more important. The exercises in this chapter were designed with the workplace in mind.

SOME KEY STRATEGIES

The following strategies are designed not only to protect you from the narcissist's toxins but also to make you a valued employee who is less likely to be dismissed from your job due to fallout from the narcissist.

If Possible, Avoid the Offender

Perhaps the most obvious way to deal with one-way relationships at work is to simply avoid them. If there is a narcissist in the lunchroom, eat somewhere else. If she is in payroll, avoid payroll. This may not be easy because people are drawn to narcissists, and there is usually a lot of action whenever they are around. Narcissists like to be seen as movers and shakers, and being around them often fills a need within us to be a part of it all. It makes us feel energized and important. Plus, narcissists always have some way of drawing you in. Remember though, narcissists are like Las Vegas: a lot of flashing bright lights with tons of excitement, but you usually walk away the loser. Better to stay away if you can.

Develop Talking Points and Stick to Them

Take a lesson from politicians. When you are in a position where you have to interact with a narcissistic coworker, rehearse the discussion as much as you can beforehand. Have a strategy. Know exactly what you want to achieve and stick to that. Don't let the narcissist suck you in to his own agendas or distract you with flattery. Politely acknowledge his agendas and get right back to your talking points. And keep the list of talking points short, two or three at most.

Stay in Your Lane

Another simple yet often overlooked strategy is to simply do your job. We believe that this is always the best work strategy. Being known to your employer as a good and conscientious employee will protect you from the slings and arrows aimed at you by narcissistic coworkers. Don't get involved in the office gossip about or with narcissistic people. If the narcissist invites you to do something outside the office, such as playing golf, politely decline. If the narcissist asks you to do special favors, simply say you are too busy doing your work. If she starts denigrating another of your coworkers, excuse yourself and go back to your job. It may take a while, but eventually the narcissist will get the picture and troll for attention elsewhere. And don't forget that when you stay in your lane, do your work, and resist the bait ("Wow, you'd make a great addition to my political action committee!"), you are supporting your organization's goals, which makes you an invaluable employee who is worth protecting. Even from narcissists.

Don't Get Taken in by the Flattery

Remember the process of splitting? After the narcissist adores you, he hates you. The narcissist will flatter the heck out of you in the beginning, projecting his fantasies of perfection onto you. If you have something that is valuable to him, he will think that you are wonderful. If you accept the flattery, you will have opened the door to a relationship. When the narcissist inevitably finds out that you are only human, he will become disappointed and then will totally devalue you, and you will be persona non grata. So don't be deceived by the flattery in the first place.

Look for Possible End Runs

If a narcissistic coworker is someone whom you have to work with or go through on a regular basis, sometimes you may choose to go around and not through her. For example, suppose you are doing a report with a narcissistic coworker who is grandstanding and wasting time by trying to expand her portion of the report. Rather than telling her to speed it up and risk a vitriolic and self-serving attack about how you cannot appreciate all the wonderful things she is putting into the report, go to the narcissist's boss and ask the boss to ask your coworker to speed things up.

It helps to be a strong networker and to cultivate relationships with others who may have more influence over the narcissist than you do. You may be able to find common ground in your organization with key individuals. Although someone might be three layers of management above you, that person is your equal if the two of you attend the same church, collect and have an affection for old vinyl records, or belong to the local Rotary Club. Maybe you have a mutual friend. It would be very difficult, indeed, for your narcissistic boss to abuse his boss's outside-of-work associate, that being you!

Also, don't forget the strategy of going over someone's head. While we do not feel that this is a good strategy to use all the time, it is certainly handy when used strategically.

Never Get into a Pissing Contest

Believe us, you will not get credit for winning a pissing match with a coworker. And in the process, you will look like as big a blowhard as the narcissist. Plus, when you get angry, you are making it personal, which lets the narcissist into your life. You really only need to state your point once or twice. Thereafter, your effort is fruitless. And never lose your temper; always stay calm. Let your narcissistic coworker know that you are off-limits and someone with whom it does not pay to argue. (Careful now: If your pride will not let you back off, you might need to examine some of your own narcissism!)

Document When Necessary

Narcissists are notorious for making big promises without necessarily feeling a need to follow through, especially if it becomes inconvenient later on. ("I just want to let you know how much we appreciate you around here. See that new office going in on the first floor? That'll be yours by the summertime, and that's a promise!") If you receive a promise from a narcissistic administrator, you will want to send an e-mail thanking the narcissist for the promise and save a copy for yourself. Consider copying others who might be key in the decision.

Also, document what the narcissist falsely claims she cannot do. For example, if your narcissistic administrator says, "Sorry, it's really not my job to review your expense account," send her an e-mail telling her that you appreciate the information, but you believe it to be incorrect. Keep a diary including dates, times, and places and exactly what the narcissist has said. Narcissists are notorious for misrepresenting events to make themselves look better. Be sure to keep other important documents, such as audits and time sheets. If you are forced to meet with a narcissist, consider bringing a witness.

Network, Network, Network

Networking always makes good sense, even when you are not dealing with a narcissistic coworker. And if you do have a narcissistic coworker, that person will think twice before taking you on if he knows you have friends and connections. Here are some good ways to go about building up your social network.

◆ Become enthusiastic about other people's agendas. Pick agendas that you believe in and those of people whom you would like to know better.

◆ Identify and make connections with rising stars and become a promoter of the star's talents. Consider training or mentoring someone new to the office. Experienced people often overlook newcomers. And, hey, this person might be your boss someday.

◆ Toot your own horn. Sometimes it is easy to get lost in the gigantic shadows that narcissists cast. While it may seem self-serving, it is a good public relations strategy to let the public know about the good things that you do. You can do this informally through the grapevine or through other, more conventional information channels. Some volunteer positions are more visible than others, and you should consider taking those that are.

◆ Be mindful of existing social networks. In just about every organization, there is a tacit social organization not portrayed on the organizational diagram. Even though they are far apart within the organization, the guy on the loading dock might be the vice president's brother-in-law and best friend, for example. It's important not to step on anyone's toes, and it's important to develop friendships across the various levels of your organization. You can do this by joining one of the extracurricular activities that many organizations offer their employees or simply by having a cup of coffee with someone you'd like to get to know.

◆ Join professional organizations. Don't overlook these. Try to attend the regular meetings and go to workshops as well. Stay fresh and informed. It will make you a valuable source of information and also help keep your batteries charged.

◆ Use the Internet. Networking websites for professionals such as LinkedIn make it easier to connect with people who have similar positions to yours as well as people who can be helpful to your career. You can also use the Internet to get more information about narcissistic and other toxic coworkers. We maintain a site at http://thetoxiccoworker .wordpress.com. Check it out!

Get a Mentor

Wisdom is a precious commodity. Find somebody within or outside of your organization who not only can help you with your career but also knows how to manage people like your narcissistic coworker. And now, with the advent of Skype, you can be mentored by anyone in the world. Pay your mentor if you have to. It's worth it.

Bloom in Your Own Garden

Be known throughout your organization as the expert in your area. Be the go-to guy or gal. Being a highly valued employee is one of the best ways to protect yourself from self-centered, self-serving others. Here are a few ways to do that:

◆ Make public presentations. Others in the organization might benefit from your knowledge and experiences. Corporations are always planning meetings or workshops. Volunteer for one and shine!

◆ Make yourself an expert in a particular area: the one who knows PowerPoint or Excel, the one who has good relationships with suppliers and customers, the one who can fix broken computers or get a copy machine to work.

◆ Publish articles in your trade. This helps you get known outside your own organization.

Making yourself indispensable to your organization and your coworkers is a great defense against the narcissist in your workplace.

Exercise Damage Control

If you are working with a narcissist, sooner or later you will need to do some damage control to repair the harm he has done to you or your reputation. Perhaps you will have to correct the false rumors that he has spread about you or the incorrect information he has given someone. If you supervise a narcissistic employee, you will have to develop a system of monitoring her on a regular basis, ensuring that she does not exploit others or inappropriately cross boundaries. Don't let these things fester; jump on them right away.

Utilize Corporate and Legal Services to Protect You

Many corporations have policies, and there are federal and state laws as well, designed to protect people from coworkers or bosses who inflict harm on others. Many corporations offer mediation services to help resolve workplace difficulties. You can contact your department of human resources to find out if these services exist in your organization.

Many states have anti-bullying laws. Workplace bullying can be defined as continual aggressive or unreasonable behavior that is humiliating to a coworker or subordinate. Workplace bullying can be physical or psychological. Also, remember that if you report the behavior of a narcissist in your workplace, many states now have laws in place to protect you from retaliation, such as New Jersey's Conscientious Employee Protection Act (CEPA), also referred to as the "whistleblower statute."

Retaliation can take many forms, such as being harassed, demoted, or "overlooked" for a promotion, or even being fired. The U.S. Equal Employment Opportunity Commission exists to protect people from racial and sexual discriminatory behaviors, which are often exhibited by narcissists. If you are confused over what avenue to take, contact an attorney who specializes in workplace law. The attorney can help guide you through the legal morass and get you the help you need.

If a narcissist is having a negative effect on you, chances are you are not alone. When narcissists are in charge, organizations do not run well. There tends to be high staff turnover, along with low morale and low productivity. Working for or with a narcissist results in a lot of stress within organizations as evidenced by increased stress-related physical and emotional disorders. This in turn leads to increased use of sick leave and absenteeism. Disciplinary actions become more frequent, as do requests for transfers. Interpersonal conflict increases among employees. Dealing with narcissistic supervisors effectively is not only good for you but is good for others as well.

Choose Your Battles

Dealing with a narcissistic boss or administrator effectively can be a huge challenge, and it's always important to pick your battles. Elsewhere we've emphasized the importance of setting boundaries and saying no and have given you examples of how to do this with a narcissistic boss (see chapter 6). However, there are instances when narcissists won't take no for an answer and will lash out or act out in some way. If you have a narcissistic bully for a boss, you may want to consider looking around for other work. If that's not an option for now, however, then your goal is to survive in what unfortunately is a highly dysfunctional work situation. In that case, you'll do better if you can figure out what your boss or supervisor really wants from you (for example, does he want to control you, does she want your undying loyalty, or does he want you to admire him?) and then use this information to your advantage. Although this may sound disingenuous, if you need the job and you need to survive in this workplace, it can be a useful approach.

DEALING WITH THE HOT SPOTS

After reading this book and completing the exercises, it will be difficult for you to go back to old patterns of reacting to the narcissist. Having a deeper understanding of narcissism will change the way that you actually perceive, experience, and react to the self-centered coworker or boss in your life.

In the following exercise, you will take a hot spot—one of the worst experiences that you have had—with your narcissistic coworker or boss and describe how you interpreted the experience, how you felt, and how you behaved. You will then have a chance to describe how you would react differently if the same thing were to happen today, based on what you've learned about narcissism.

Here's an example of a hot spot: "My narcissistic secretary asked me to pick up her dry cleaning on my way home from work. She often promises me 'a special treat' if I do, hinting at a sexual relationship. I don't mind so much, but she never gives me money, and I have to use my own money and accept her offer to pay me back the next day. But she never pays me until weeks later and never reimburses me correctly. She now owes me over thirty dollars. Needless to say, I never get my 'special treat.'"

If this were you talking, your past interpretations or personal beliefs about the hot spot might be "Everybody adores her. She is the office hottie, and we all want to be her favorite. I was hoping that she would like me. I thought it would make me feel special and the office staff would look up to me. I was hoping that she would really find me attractive."

You might say that you felt the following: "I felt used and stupid, like a hormonal teenager in heat. I feel like the office fool. I feel unattractive and awkward, like I am the ultimate loser."

Here's how you might describe your behavior: "I told her continuously that it was okay if she didn't have all the money, in spite of the fact that I knew I could use the money I'd loaned her. I lied when she asked me if I still adored her and I said yes. I laughed at her dumb jokes and acted like I was really interested in her long-winded story about how the guys at the laundry fell all over themselves when she told them about her sexy dresses at home. I acted in a way that was totally not me, a fake, a phony."

Given what you know about narcissism now, you might have a very different reaction: "If the same thing happened today, I would tell her to go elsewhere for a loan."

Exercise: Your Hot Spot

Now describe one of your own hot spots and how you thought, felt, and behaved at the time. Then describe how you would reinterpret the same situation if it were to happen today, given what you now know about narcissism. How would you respond to the narcissist?

Your hot spot:

_____

_____

_____

_____

Your interpretations or your personal beliefs about the hot spot were:

_____

_____

_____

_____

How did you feel? List your emotions:

_____

_____

_____

_____

How did you behave? Write down how you responded:

_____

_____

_____

_____

Now that you know about narcissism, how would you interpret the same situation differently? How would you react differently if the same thing were to happen now?

_____

_____

_____

_____

_____

_____

===

Writing about your hot spots can be instructive. If you have other hot spots that you want to reinterpret, you can write about what happened in the past and consider how you might react differently now and in the future if something similar were to occur. This will prepare you for reacting differently to the narcissist in your workplace. It will also be rewarding to recognize how much you've learned and how far you've already come.

ABOVE AND BEYOND: DIFFERENTIATION OF SELF

This part of this chapter goes above and beyond simple problem solving into the much more complex and challenging task of not just changing what you do but transforming who you are and how you approach life in general: a challenging and continuing process of self-improvement which can take years. While it is beyond the scope of this chapter to give full instruction in this area, we want to introduce you to the concepts here as a real and effective solution to workplace issues. We think you will find the ideas that follow very useful in dealing with your narcissistic coworker.

◆ A Colleague's Story

One day, as we were walking across campus, we were observing staff taking care of the beautiful campus surroundings when we came across a colleague who went into a tirade about how the college wasted too *much money on campus care and maintenance. This was an obvious overreaction, and it seemed to upset this colleague for the rest of the day. Observing this overreaction, a coworker observed under his breath, "Dude, get a life."*

Actually, our coworker wasn't very far from wrong. Our mutual colleague needs to be able to separate himself from some of the day-to-day activities of his job and not let everything that goes on at the campus bleed into him and totally disrupt his sense of calm. That is, he needs to differentiate what truly matters to him from the smaller things that go on in his job and only respond to the ones that could really affect him.

In the same way that it is possible to become enmeshed or codependent with another person, it is also possible to become enmeshed or codependent with your workplace and fellow workers. People who are overly dependent upon their workplace will naturally be more affected by job stressors than people who are not, and this includes being stressed out by a narcissistic coworker. We are not saying here that you should be unconcerned about the issues that affect you at work; rather, we are saying that you should not let them consume you. If your whole life centers around your job, narcissistic coworkers will wear you out in a hurry. If, on the other hand, other things are important to you, such as working with a charity that brings food to needy and hungry children, for example, you will probably not spend as much time rehashing old memories of the times your self-centered coworker used you or got the best of you.

By now, you should understand the importance of maintaining boundaries. One of the simplest and most basic of all boundaries is the ability to recognize which things hold the most value in your life and which don't. Psychologists often refer to this ability to discern what's important from what's not as *differentiation of self*. When you become overly enmeshed in your workplace, you lack this differentiation of self. This is referred to as *fusion*. People who are fused with their workplace, like the man who complained about campus maintenance, are much more disturbed by what happens on their job than people who are not fused.

One of the more recent trends in resolving interpersonal issues at work has been to examine how our early relationships with family members may affect our relationships on the job. In other words, you may find that in the workplace you repeat patterns of behavior that you learned while growing up.

Our first attempts at self-differentiation originate when we are growing up and are trying to separate our own intellectual and emotional functioning from that of our family. When we are very young, naturally everything that goes on in the family affects us, and we cannot help but be affected by our parents' behavior. It is natural to be fused when we are children. As we get older, we begin to develop our own identities and differentiate ourselves from our family, having more separate lives of our own. We should no longer be fused with our family.

When people grow up and become employed, those who are high in self-differentiation are able to maintain their sense of well-being, even when things around them are falling apart. They feel insulated and do not become entangled in the emotional upsets or problems of others. They know who they are and embrace their own personal values strongly, and it is difficult to knock them off course. On the other hand, people who are low in self-differentiation are like cars without shock absorbers and feel every bump in the road; everything seems to upset them. They let everything in, like houses with no walls. (So the next time your boss tells you that everyone there "is just one big happy family," consider what she is actually saying!)

We have created a scale to measure your degree of fusion to your workplace. Don't imagine that anyone is perfect in this area; they aren't. But as a general rule, lower scores on this scale are best. They would indicate that a person is high in self-differentiation and low in fusion.

Exercise: Workplace Differentiation Inventory

The following list of statements takes an inventory of your feelings and thoughts about your work and your relationships with supervisors and coworkers (including people you supervise). Please read each statement carefully and then, on a scale of 1 to 6, where 1 signifies that this statement is not at all true of you and 6 signifies that it is very true of you, circle the number that best describes how well the statement describes you. There are no right or wrong answers.

1. "I have few interests and hobbies outside of work." 1 2 3 4 5 6

2. "Coworkers or administrators make me feel frustrated." 1 2 3 4 5 6

3. "I don't seem to handle job stress well." 1 2 3 4 5 6

4. "I feel emotionally overwhelmed at work." 1 2 3 4 5 6

5. "I wish I were less emotionally reactive at my job." 1 2 3 4 5 6

6. "If I won the lottery, the first thing I would do is quit my job." 1 2 3 4 5 6

7. "I often feel that I like my work, but I dislike my coworkers." 1 2 3 4 5 6

8. "I react strongly to negative performance evaluations at work." 1 2 3 4 5 6

9. "I often feel that my supervisors or coworkers demand too much from me." 1 2 3 4 5 6

10. "If I've had an argument at work, I have trouble letting go of it." 1 2 3 4 5 6

11. "Overall, I'm not very satisfied and content with my job." 1 2 3 4 5 6

12. "I don't get along well with most people I work with." 1 2 3 4 5 6

13. "I feel my job burnout is the result of stressful interactions with supervisors or coworkers." 1 2 3 4 5 6

14. "If I've had an argument or disagreement with a coworker, I'll often have trouble sleeping at night."　　1　2　3　4　5　6

15. "I am very committed to my work, but I often feel that coworkers are not as committed or dedicated as I am."　　1　2　3　4　5　6

16. "I find myself thinking a lot about things that happen at work even when I'm at home."　　1　2　3　4　5　6

17. "I often feel very unappreciated in my job or career."　　1　2　3　4　5　6

18. "When it comes to my job, it's true that if you want something done right, you have to do it yourself."　　1　2　3　4　5　6

19. "The thing that stresses me out most about work is the fear of not doing a good job."　　1　2　3　4　5　6

20. "I feel my work is my whole life."　　1　2　3　4　5　6

21. "It seems that I live to work and work to live."　　1　2　3　4　5　6

22. "I tend to take my work problems home with me."　　1　2　3　4　5　6

23. "My job is the most important thing in my life."　　1　2　3　4　5　6

24. "When I am away from my job, I feel I have nothing else to do."　　1　2　3　4　5　6

Now add up your score. How did you do? We believe that people who score 50 and below are far less fused with issues that occur in their workplace, including those involving narcissistic coworkers. If you are in this group, congratulations! You are much less prone to be affected by a narcissistic coworker. If you scored between 51 and 75 points, a good deal of your happiness in life comes from outside your workplace, but there may be times when you overreact to workplace issues. You most likely need to make some minor adjustments in your life, and a little self-differentiation might help. If you scored over 75 but under 100 points, perhaps you are too involved with your work and need to begin to discover more things that you value, both in your workplace and, if possible, in other areas of your life. And if you scored over 100 points, it is most likely that you are disturbed about a number of problems in your workplace besides a narcissistic coworker. Developing your own personal values and goals both within and outside of the workplace is going to be essential for you in overcoming workplace stresses. You might need to make this a high priority in your life.

DEVELOPING YOUR OWN CAREER VALUES AND GOALS

Focusing on your own values and goals is always a good idea. When you are proactive about your own career, you will find it easier to insulate yourself from the narcissist's tactics. You will have more self-differentiation. Putting your energy into what you most value about your work will help you to be not so easily derailed by the narcissist's insensitive incursions. Here are some examples of how that might work:

◆ It will be easier to avoid being sucked into the narcissist's request that you participate in his new moneymaking pyramid scheme because you are taking extra classes, for example, to make you a more marketable employee.

◆ You will turn down the narcissist's invitations more easily because you are focused on your upcoming bid for a promotion that will look wonderful on your resume.

◆ You will soar above the narcissist's venomous rants about the "inefficiency of the supply room," knowing that others are looking up to you as a leader with character, something you always wanted to achieve.

Being clearheaded and passionate about what you want to achieve in your career puts daily difficulties into perspective. It helps you outgrow the traps of the narcissist in much the same way you outgrew schoolyard teasing or bullying. In fact, there's probably not much difference between these situations. Try to rise above the fray by aiming for the higher things in life.

So, what do you want out of life in terms of your career? What goals do you want to set for yourself? Remember also that it's important to specify when you want to achieve your goals, or else they are just dreams and fantasies.

Exercise: Identifying Your Career Values and Goals

This is a three-part exercise. First, identify your long-term goals. These might include any of the following: in five years, you want to be making $200,000 a year; by this time next year, you want to be branch supervisor; you want to have a $20,000 down payment to put on a house in six months; you want to train someone to take over your position by the summer so you can accept a transfer opportunity to Boulder; you want to be number one in sales this quarter; you want to have enough money to retire in six years; you want to be able to take a month off next year to take your family to China; you want to go back for a master's degree so you can become a manager. Use your imagination to come up with your own long-term goals and be specific about when you want to achieve them.

What are your long-term goals?

_____

_____

_____

What are your short-term goals? Write down what you would need to do in the next few months to put yourself on the right track for achieving your long-term goals. Specify dates for achieving these short-term goals.

Date: _____ Short-term goal: _____

Date: _____ Short-term goal: _____

Date: _____ Short-term goal: _____

What are your daily goals? What would you need to do today and this week to help forward your short-term goals?

_____

_____

_____

_____

Again, defining and developing your own career values and goals is a great way to overcome stresses on the job, especially those created by a narcissistic coworker.

Certainly, there is no shortage of self-serving individuals in the workplace today. Knowing how to manage them and ward off their attacks is a fundamental job skill. This chapter has given you many good tools to help you in this endeavor. Remember, change doesn't happen overnight, and most likely your narcissistic coworker will not change. But if you are persistent in your application of these tools, you will be able to survive and perhaps even thrive in your workplace.

A final note: If you are in a truly toxic environment, you might find it in your own best interest to leave and find work elsewhere. After all, no one should have to sacrifice her health and well-being just to stay employed at a particular place. Remember, even in tough economic times, those who work the hardest at finding gainful and meaningful employment are still usually the ones who get the best positions. If you find yourself in a highly toxic workplace, perhaps you should consider putting your energies elsewhere. This option is always open to you.

Resources

RECOMMENDED READING

Bowen, M. *Family Therapy in Clinical Practice*. Lanham, MD: Jason Aronson, 1992.

Brown, N. *Children of the Self-Absorbed: A Grown-Up's Guide to Getting Over Narcissistic Parents*. Oakland, CA: New Harbinger Publications, 2001.

———. *Loving the Self-Absorbed*. Oakland, CA: New Harbinger Publications, 2003.

Carter, S., and J. Sokol. *Help, I'm in Love with a Narcissist*. New York: M. Evans and Co., 2005.

Doherty, N., and M. Guyler. *The Essential Guide to Workplace Mediation and Conflict Resolution*. Philadelphia: Kogan Page, 2008.

Forward, S., with D. Frazier. *Emotional Blackmail*. New York: Harper Paperbacks, 1998.

Glass, L. *Toxic People: Ten Ways of Dealing with People Who Make Your Life Miserable*. New York: St. Martin's Press, 1995.

Glowinski, K. *Narcissistic Personality Disorder*. N.p.: BookSurge Publishing. 2008.

Ilardo, J. *Risk-Taking for Personal Growth*. Oakland, CA: New Harbinger Publications, 1992.

Mooney, N. *I Can't Believe She Did That! Why Women Betray Other Women at Work*. New York: St. Martin's Press, 1970.

Payson, E. *The Wizard of Oz and Other Narcissists*. Royal Oak, MI: Julian Day Publications, 2002.

Ronningstam, E. *Disorders of Narcissism: Diagnostic, Clinical, and Empirical Implications*. Washington, DC: American Psychiatric Press, 1998.

Rothstein, A. *The Narcissistic Pursuit of Perfection*. 2nd rev. ed. Madison, CT: International Universities Press, 1999.

Simon, G. K. *In Sheep's Clothing: Understanding and Dealing with Manipulative People*. New York: A. J Christopher and Co., 1996.

Stenack, R. *Stop Controlling Me! What to Do When Someone You Love Has Too Much Power Over You*. Oakland, CA: New Harbinger Publications, 2001.

Vaknin, S., and L. Rangelovska. *Malignant Self-Love and Narcissism Revisited*. Prague, CZ: Narcissus Publications, 2007.

Viscusi, S. *Bulletproof Your Job*. New York: HarperCollins, 2008.

Zayn, C., and K. Dibble. *Narcissist Lovers: How to Cope, Recover and Move On*. Fall Hills, NJ: New Horizon Press, 2007.

OTHER RESOURCES

Institute for Advance Studies in Personality and Psychopathology. www.millon.net.

The institute is run by Theodore Millon, a noted expert in narcissism and personality disorders; it trains clinicians who treat narcissistic people and is a good starting place to ask for a recommendation for a therapist who can set up a personal intervention.

Personality Disorders Institute, Weill Medical College, Cornell University. www.borderlinedisorders.com.

The home of Otto Kernberg, one of the leaders in personality disorder research, this institute trains psychotherapists to treat "difficult patients," including narcissists, and offers help to those afflicted with personality disorders.

References

Akhtar, S. 2009. Love, sex, and marriage in the setting of pathological narcissism. *Psychiatric Annals* 39:185–190.

Akhtar, S., and A. J. Thomson. 1982. Overview: Narcissistic personality disorder. *American Journal of Psychiatry* 139:12–20.

American Psychiatric Association. 2000. *Diagnostic and Statistical Manual of Mental Disorders*. 4th ed., text rev. Washington, DC: American Psychiatric Association.

Beattie, M. 1987. *Codependent No More: How to Stop Controlling Others and Start Caring for Yourself.* New York: HarperCollins.

———. 1989. *Beyond Codependency: And Getting Better All the Time.* New York: HarperCollins.

Behary, W. T. 2008. *Disarming the Narcissist: Surviving and Thriving with the Self-Absorbed.* Oakland, CA: New Harbinger Publications.

Bernstein, A. J. 2001. *Emotional Vampires: Dealing with People Who Drain You Dry.* New York: McGraw-Hill.

———. 2003. *How to Deal with Emotionally Explosive People.* New York: McGraw-Hill.

Black, J., and G. Enns. 1997. *Better Boundaries: Owning and Treasuring Your Own Life.* Oakland, CA: New Harbinger Publications.

Campbell, W. K. 2005. *When You Love a Man Who Loves Himself.* Naperville, IL: Sourcebooks Casablanca.

Cavaiola, A., and N. Lavender. 2000. *Toxic Coworkers: How to Deal with Dysfunctional People on the Job.* Oakland, CA: New Harbinger Publications.

Freud, S. 1914. On narcissism: An introduction. In *The Standard Edition of the Complete Psychological Works of Sigmund Freud,* ed. and trans. J. Strachey, 14:69–102. London: Hogarth Press, 1953.

Harris, T. A. 1967. *I'm Okay, You're Okay.* New York: HarperCollins.

Hendrix, H. 1988. *Getting the Love You Want: A Guide for Couples.* New York: Harper and Row.

Horney, K. 1991. *Neurosis and Human Growth: The Struggle Towards Self-Realization.* New York: W. W. Norton

Hotchkiss, S. 2002. *Why Is It Always About You? The Seven Deadly Sins of Narcissism.* New York: Free Press.

Martinez-Lewi, L. 2008. *Freeing Yourself from the Narcissist in Your Life.* New York: Penguin Group.

Maslow, A. H. 1970. *Motivation and Personality.* 2nd ed. New York: Harper and Row.

Miller, S. D., and I. K. Berg. 1995. *The Miracle Method: A Radically New Approach to Problem Drinking.* New York: W. W. Norton

Millon, T., with R. D. Davis. 1996. *Disorders of Personality: DSM-IV and Beyond.* New York: John Wiley and Sons.

Reich, A. 1960. Pathologic forms of self-esteem regulation. *Psychoanalytic Study of the Child* 15:215–232.

Ronningstam, E. 2005. *Identifying and Understanding the Narcissistic Personality.* New York: Oxford University Press.

Walker, L. E. 2000. *The Battered Woman Syndrome.* 2nd ed. New York: Springer Publishing.

Neil J. Lavender, Ph.D., has worked as a practicing psychologist specializing in relationship problems since 1989. He is professor of psychology at Ocean County College in the Jersey Shore area. Along with Alan Cavaiola, he coauthored *Toxic Coworkers*, which presently has been translated into five languages. Together, they have been featured on the radio, on television, and in print media addressing the topic of personality disorders in personal and workplace relationships.

Alan Cavaiola, Ph.D., is professor in the Department of Psychological Counseling at Monmouth University where he is a member of the graduate faculty. He is a licensed psychologist, a licensed clinical alcohol and drug counselor, and a licensed professional counselor. In addition to his teaching, Cavaiola has been a practicing psychologist since 1988. He is coauthor of *Toxic Coworkers*, *Assessment and Treatment of DWI Offenders*, and *A Practical Guide to Crisis Intervention*.

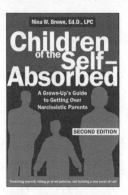

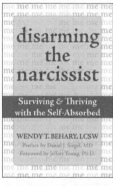